RUSSIA

ABDO
Publishing Company

RUSSIA

by Andrea Pelleschi

Content Consultant
William Benton Whisenhunt, Professor of History
College of DuPage

CREDITS

Published by ABDO Publishing Company, PO Box 398166, Minneapolis, MN 55439.
Copyright © 2013 by Abdo Consulting Group, Inc. International copyrights reserved
in all countries. No part of this book may be reproduced in any form without written
permission from the publisher. The Essential Library™ is a trademark and logo of
ABDO Publishing Company.

Printed in the United States of America,
North Mankato, Minnesota
112012
012013

Editor: Lisa Owings
Series Designer: Emily Love

About the Author: Andrea Pelleschi has been writing and editing children's books for
more than 12 years. She has a master's of fine arts in creative writing from Emerson
College and has taught writing classes for college freshmen. She currently lives in
Cincinnati, Ohio, and hopes to travel to Russia someday.

Cataloging-in-Publication Data

Pelleschi, Andrea.
 Russia / Andrea Pelleschi.
   p. cm. -- (Countries of the world)
Includes bibliographical references and index.
ISBN 978-1-61783-635-0
1. Russia (Federation)--Juvenile literature. 2. Russia--Juvenile literature. 3. Soviet Union-
-Juvenile literature.   I. Title.
947--dc22

2012946083

**Cover: This beautiful wooden palace in Moscow, Russia,
was once the home of Tsar Alexis I.**

TABLE OF CONTENTS

CHAPTER 1
A VISIT TO RUSSIA

It's time for your Russian vacation, and the travel possibilities are endless. As Russia is the largest country in the world, you could easily spend months trekking across its vastness.

You have only a week for your trip, so you start in the capital city of Moscow. Because the city's sights are spread out, you use the metro, Moscow's ornately decorated subway system, to get from place to place.

Your first stop is Red Square in the oldest section of Moscow. This large open area was established in the fifteenth century and has seen everything from market stalls and parades to executions and riots. Even military tanks once rolled over its cobblestones.

Today it gives you an awe-inspiring view of the Cathedral of Saint Basil the Blessed. With its nine domes

The Park Pobedy Station in the metro has the longest escalator in the world.

The Cathedral of Saint Basil the Blessed is the highlight of Moscow's Red Square.

7

painted in whimsical patterns of red, green, blue, and gold, the church looks like something straight out of a fairy tale.

Other distinctive buildings include the stark-white GUM department store with its intricately carved facade, as well as the red-spired State Historical Museum. The simplest building is the mausoleum of Vladimir Lenin, founder of the Soviet Union. Its blocky red and black exterior houses Lenin's body, still preserved from the time of his death in 1924.

The largest structure next to the square is an enormous red brick wall with towers and spires, similar to the outer wall of a castle. Behind the wall, you can see the roofs of palaces, churches, and other buildings. This complex is the Kremlin, and it houses the original center of the Russian government.

After touring Red Square, you head west to the winding pedestrian streets of the Arbat for a taste of old Russia. As you walk, you see artists

THE KREMLIN

A kremlin is a type of a walled fortress found in many Russian cities. It typically has towers, moats, and other defensive structures built into its walls. Once you step past the gate, you'll find palaces, churches, government offices, and armories. The Moscow Kremlin is no exception. Originally built in 1156 out of wood, this triangular fortress has housed the center of the Russian church and government for most of its existence. In the fifteenth century, Ivan the Great rebuilt the structure with the red brick we see today.

sketching portraits, street performers playing guitars, and vendors selling Russian dolls. Hungry? The enticing smells of traditional Russian fare draw you into one of the many cafés. There, you sample beet soup called borscht and tiny dumplings called *pelmeni* filled with your choice of meat, fish, or mushrooms.

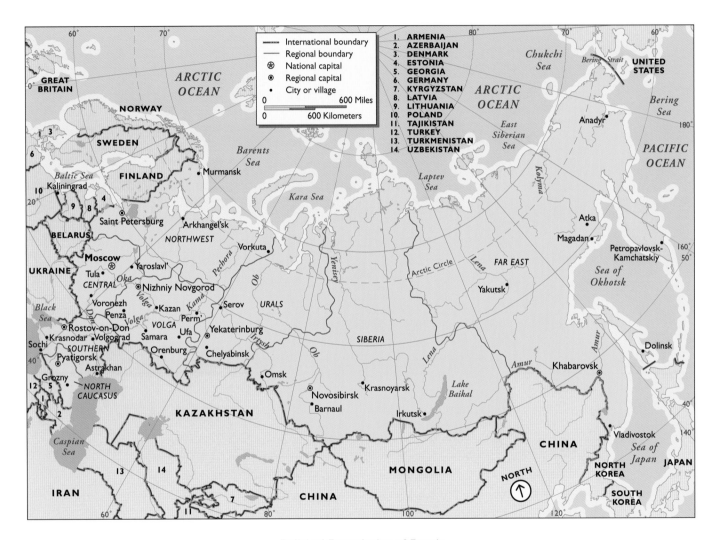

International boundary	1. ARMENIA
Regional boundary	2. AZERBAIJAN
⊛ National capital	3. DENMARK
◉ Regional capital	4. ESTONIA
• City or village	5. GEORGIA
	6. GERMANY
	7. KYRGYZSTAN
	8. LATVIA
	9. LITHUANIA
	10. POLAND
	11. TAJIKISTAN
	12. TURKEY
	13. TURKMENISTAN
	14. UZBEKISTAN

0   600 Miles
0   600 Kilometers

Political Boundaries of Russia

Finally, a quick taxi ride brings you to the opulent Sanduny Banya, where you treat yourself to a relaxing steam bath. It's the perfect end to a busy day.

A VAST COUNTRY

Russia is so large it can be hard to wrap your mind around its size. It sprawls across both Europe and Asia, taking up one-sixth of the world's landmass.[1] This means different areas of the country have vastly different geographies, climates, and cultures. Three-quarters of the population live in the western third of Russia, and it is here you'll find the modern cities of Moscow and Saint Petersburg.

If you take the Trans-Siberian Railway all the way to its last stop in the east, you'll find a less dense population. Most of the people here are part of small ethnic groups, such as the nomadic Buryat people. Others are descended from Siberian pioneers or ex-prisoners, and they have a tough, hardworking spirit. Those who live along the Pacific Ocean are

YAKUTSK

The northeastern city of Yakutsk is the coldest city in the world. Temperatures in January average -40 degrees Fahrenheit (-40°C) and can plunge more than ten degrees below that.[2] It is so cold in winter that eyeglasses can freeze to a person's skin. Yakutsk also has unusual architecture. The warmth of the buildings would cause the permafrost to melt if they sat directly on the ground, making the buildings collapse, so they are all on stilts. But Yakutsk's cold is great for fossil hunters. Some of the world's best-preserved mammoths have been found there.

isolated from the central government in Moscow and have come to be self-reliant.

The polar region of the far north has a long, harsh winter and permafrost, or permanently frozen ground. The people here can't farm the land, so they make their living by hunting, fishing, mining, or herding.

In the south, you'll find more than 100 ethnic groups, such as the nomadic Kalmyk who live in tents called yurts and raise horses, cattle, sheep, and goats. There are also the Tatars, Kazakhs, Uzbeks, Bashkirs, and many more.

RUSSIAN HOSPITALITY

A common characteristic of all Russians is their hospitality. Don't be surprised if you get invited to someone's home for a quick snack or a

The Chukchi people inhabit the northeasternmost region of Siberia.

Russians are known for their hospitality.

leisurely meal. Even Russians who don't have much to share will insist on giving you all they have. If you're invited to eat at the kitchen table, then you have become a good friend with the host.

If you get invited to a party, never shake hands across the doorway. It is considered bad luck. And if you bring flowers, always bring an odd number. Bouquets with even numbers of flowers are strictly for funerals. If someone raises a glass and toasts you with the words "Za zdorovje," know they are wishing you the best of health.

[SNAPSHOT]

Official name: Russian Federation

Capital city: Moscow

Form of government: federation

Title of leaders: president (head of state); prime minister (head of government)

Currency: ruble

Population (July 2012 est.): 142,517,670
World rank: 9

Size: 6,601,668 square miles (17,098,242 sq km)
World rank: 1

Language: Russian

Official religion (if any): none

Per capita GDP (2011, US dollars): $17,000
World rank: 71

CHAPTER 2
GEOGRAPHY: WORLD'S LARGEST COUNTRY

With an area of 6,601,668 square miles (17,098,242 sq km), Russia is the largest country in the world.[1] It stretches from the Baltic Sea in eastern Europe, across northern Asia, and out to the Pacific Ocean in the east. Canada, the world's second-largest country, doesn't even come close. Russia is almost twice its size.[2]

With so much land, Russia's environment varies greatly from deserts to semiarid grassy plains and from Arctic tundra to deep forests. It contains the longest river and largest lake in Europe, as well as the highest and lowest points in Europe.

Much of Russia has only two seasons: winter and summer.

The Volga River, Europe's longest, comes together with the Oka River east of Moscow at Nizhniy Novgorod, Russia.

In the west, Russia shares borders with the countries of Estonia, Finland, Norway, Latvia, Belarus, and Ukraine. Georgia and Azerbaijan lie to the southwest. Russia's southern neighbors are Kazakhstan, China, Mongolia, and North Korea. The oblast, or province, of Kaliningrad is isolated from the rest of the country; it lies to the west between Poland and Lithuania. It was annexed from Germany after World War II (1939–1945).

REGIONS AND LAND FORMATIONS

Russia can be divided into regions based on geographic features. The Kola-Karelian region in northwestern Russia has icy plateaus and low ridges interspersed with lakes and marshes.

In western Russia, the Russian Plateau extends east from Europe to the Ural Mountains and south to the Caucasus Mountains. This broad plain contains both the highest and lowest points in Europe. Mount Elbrus, an extinct volcano in the Caucasus Mountains, rises to 18,480 feet (5,633 m).[3] Near the Caspian Sea, the land dips to 92 feet (28 m) below sea level.[4]

The Ural Mountains and the lowlands surrounding them form another region in Russia. This low mountain range is the dividing line between the continents of Europe and Asia. Most of the

The summit of Mount Elbrus is the highest point in Europe.

KAMCHATKA VOLCANOES

Sometimes called the "land of fire and ice," the Kamchatka Peninsula has almost 130 volcanoes, 22 of which are currently active.[8] These volcanoes are part of a long, curving chain of volcanoes—called the Ring of Fire—that encircles the Pacific Ocean. Besides volcanoes, the peninsula also boasts boiling mud pools, ice crevices that spew volcanic vapor, mineral springs, and dozens of geysers.

peaks rise between just 3,000 and 5,000 feet (900 and 1,500 m).[5]

The West Siberian Plain takes up approximately one-seventh of Russia's land, running west to east from the Ural Mountains to the Yenisey River.[6] It consists of floodplains and swamps at a low elevation. Moving east from there is the Central Siberian Plateau and then the Lena Plateau. Mountain ranges cover most of the area between the Lena River and the Pacific, including the Stanovoy Range, the Kolyma Mountains, and the Verkhoyansk Mountains.

Southeastern Russia is punctuated by high mountain ranges, some of which line the southern boundary of the country, including the Altai, Western, Eastern, and Sayan Mountains. The Kamchatka Peninsula in the northeast corner of the country contains numerous volcanoes.

RIVERS AND LAKES

Six of the world's 50 longest rivers wind through Russia.[7] In the north, four of them flow into the Arctic Ocean: the Yenisey, Lena, Ob, and

Legend:
- — · — International boundary
- ✪ National capital
- • City or village

0 _____ 600 Miles
0 _____ 600 Kilometers

- Cropland
- Pasture
- Forest
- Mountain region
- Desert
- Barren land

1. ARMENIA
2. AZERBAIJAN
3. DENMARK
4. ESTONIA
5. GEORGIA
6. GERMANY
7. KYRGYZSTAN
8. LATVIA
9. LITHUANIA
10. POLAND
11. TAJIKISTAN
12. TURKEY
13. TURKMENISTAN
14. UZBEKISTAN

Geography of Russia

Irtysh. In the south, the Amur River forms a boundary with China and drains into the Pacific Ocean. In the west, the Dnieper and Don Rivers flow into the Black Sea. The Volga, Europe's longest river, starts north of Moscow and flows south to the Caspian Sea. This river is 2,193 miles (3,530 km) long.[9]

VOLGA RIVER

Russian civilization is thought to have begun along the Volga, Europe's longest river. Coined "Mother Volga" in Russian folklore, the river starts as a small stream north of Moscow in the Valdai Hills. By the time it empties into the Caspian Sea, it has absorbed approximately 151,000 streams and rivers into its system.[13] Today, reservoirs and dams interrupt the river's flow, turning it into a series of man-made lakes. The dams generate electricity for hydroelectric plants, but they also divert water away from the river. This threatens fish habitats, resulting in a decline of fisheries in the Volga. It has also reduced the water level of the Caspian Sea, which has been gradually dropping since 1930.

Russia has approximately 2 million lakes.[10] Lake Ladoga, Europe's largest lake, is near Saint Petersburg. Lake Baikal in the Asian section of Russia is the world's deepest lake and the largest freshwater lake by volume.[11]

The Caspian Sea in southwestern Russia is the world's largest salt lake and the largest inland body of water. It is larger than the country of Japan.[12]

CLIMATE AND SEASONS

Russia is located so far north, with a long coastline on the chilly Arctic Ocean, that some parts of the country remain below freezing for much of the year. In fact, rivers in northern Siberia can stay frozen for 250 days at a time.[14]

This means most of Russia faces long, cold winters that turn quickly to summer with almost no spring. In the fall, most of the country cools down just as quickly. Summers are brief but warm.

Russia's polar north has a tundra climate with below-freezing average temperatures and low precipitation. The area north of 66.6 degrees latitude—approximately one-fifth of Russia—is within the Arctic Circle, where on some winter days the sun never rises.[15] Those who live south of the tundra experience a subarctic

LAKE BAIKAL

At 25 million years old and with a maximum depth of 5,577 feet (1,700 m), Lake Baikal is the oldest and deepest freshwater lake in the world.[16] Located in southeast Siberia, this long, skinny lake is filled with pure blue water. The shoreline is rocky or tree lined with picturesque mountains in the background. Approximately 1,340 species of animals and 570 species of plants live in and around the lake, including the freshwater Baikal seal, or nerpa.[17] Because of this diversity, Lake Baikal is called the "Galapagos of Russia."

AVERAGE TEMPERATURE AND PRECIPITATION

Region (City)	Average January Temperature Minimum/Maximum	Average July Temperature Minimum/Maximum	Average Precipitation January/July
Northern European (Arkhangel'sk)	15.4/2.3°F (-9.2/-16.5°C)	71.2/52.3°F (21.8/11.3°C)	1.1/2.3 inches (2.0/5.0 cm)
Western European (Moscow)	21/11°F (-6/-11°C)	71/55°F (21/12°C)	1.4/3.2 inches (3.0/8.0 cm)
Western European (Saint Petersburg)	24/15°F (-4/-9°C)	70/56°F (21/13°C)	1.1/2.6 inches (2.1/6.0 cm)
Eastern Siberia (Irkutsk)	8.8/-7.6°F (-12.9/-22°C)	76.6/55.2°F (24.8/12.9°C)	0.4/3.8 inches (1.0/9.0 cm)
Russian Far East (Yakutsk)	-31.2/-42.7°F (-35.1/-41.5°C)	77.9/54.9°F (25.5/12.7°C)	0.3/1.5 inches (0.8 cm/3.0 cm)
Russian Far East (Vladivostok)	17.6/4.5°F (-8/-15.3°C)	70.2/60.4°F (21.2/15.8°C)	0.4/4.2 inches (1.0/10.0 cm)[18]

climate: long, cold winters with little precipitation. European Russia has a humid continental climate with hot summers, cold winters, and generous precipitation throughout the year. The south has a steppe

Those who endure Russia's harsh winters are rewarded by the beauty of the aurora borealis.

climate with cold winters and hot, dry summers. Parts of southeastern Russia experience a subtropical climate where temperatures remain above freezing year-round and precipitation occurs regularly throughout the year.

SAINT PETERSBURG

In 1703, Peter the Great began building Saint Petersburg on the Baltic Sea. He named the city after his patron saint and gathered artisans and architects from all over Europe to design and build fortresses, palaces, and homes. The city was laid out in a grid pattern and using multiple architectural styles. Since the land was marshy, Saint Petersburg was subject to frequent floods. Numerous canals were built to control the flooding. More than 400 bridges had to be built over the canals, giving Saint Petersburg the nickname "Venice of the North."[19]

CITIES AND PROVINCES

Russia is divided into eight federal districts: the Northwest, Central, Southern, North Caucasus, Volga, Urals, Siberia, and Far East. The Central and Northwest districts house Moscow and Saint Petersburg, respectively. Russia's federal districts are further divided into 83 administrative regions.

Russia has more than ten cities with populations greater than 1 million people. The largest is Moscow, the capital, with a population of more than 10.5 million. The next largest is Saint Petersburg at approximately

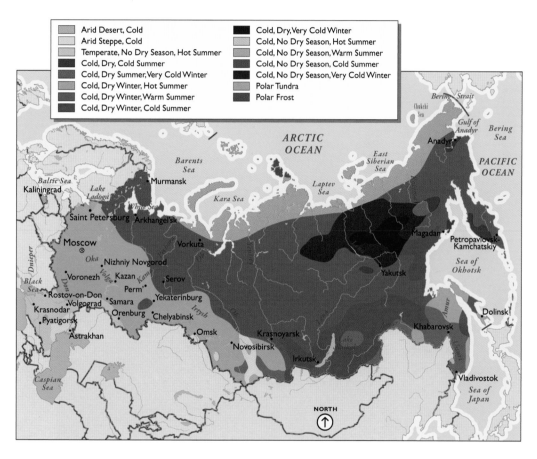

Arid Desert, Cold	Cold, Dry, Very Cold Winter
Arid Steppe, Cold	Cold, No Dry Season, Hot Summer
Temperate, No Dry Season, Hot Summer	Cold, No Dry Season, Warm Summer
Cold, Dry, Cold Summer	Cold, No Dry Season, Cold Summer
Cold, Dry Summer, Very Cold Winter	Cold, No Dry Season, Very Cold Winter
Cold, Dry Winter, Hot Summer	Polar Tundra
Cold, Dry Winter, Warm Summer	Polar Frost
Cold, Dry Winter, Cold Summer	

Climate of Russia

4.6 million. Other large cities include Novosibirsk, Yekaterinburg, and Nizhniy Novgorod, each with a population of 1.3 million or more.[20]

Russia once had 11 time zones but cut them down to nine in 2010.

The canals of Saint Petersburg invite comparisons to Venice, Italy.

CHAPTER 3

ANIMALS AND NATURE: LIVING IN THE NORTH

Russia's national animal, the brown bear, lives in Europe, Asia, and North America. Brown bears are omnivores, feeding mostly on berries, roots, small mammals, and fish. During summer and fall, they consume huge quantities of food so they can add a layer of fat to their bodies. This stored-up energy allows them to spend winters hibernating in their dens without eating. Female brown bears give birth to one to five cubs during hibernation, each weighing less than 2.2 pounds (1 kg). Most of the bears in Europe and Asia reach 48 to 83 inches (120 to 210 cm) in length and weigh 300 to 550 pounds (135 to

A brown bear can eat up to 90 pounds (40 kg) of food per day.

The mighty brown bear is a symbol of Russia.

ENDANGERED SPECIES IN RUSSIA

According to the International Union for Conservation of Nature (IUCN), Russia is home to the following numbers of species that are categorized by the organization as Critically Endangered, Endangered, or Vulnerable:

Mammals	32
Birds	49
Reptiles	8
Amphibians	0
Fishes	35
Mollusks	8
Other Invertebrates	24
Plants	13
Total	169[2]

250 kg). The Siberian brown bear is larger and can weigh as much as 800 pounds (360 kg).

ANIMALS

Russia has several bands, or belts, of terrain, each containing different animal and plant life. In the north along the Arctic Ocean is the first belt, an Arctic desert where few plants and animals can live. South of that is the tundra, a flat, treeless plain where the ground is permanently frozen. Reindeer thrive in the cold temperatures, and approximately 4 million roam this frozen land.[1] There are also Arctic foxes, wolves, musk oxen, and snowy owls. Off the Arctic coast live seals, walrus, polar bears, and whales.

Similar to the polar bear and Arctic fox, the snowy owl's white color helps it blend in with its surroundings.

South of the tundra lies the taiga, a belt of dense forest that covers approximately half of Russia. This forested region houses a wide variety of animals, including squirrels, polecats, foxes, wolverines, and sables, which are hunted for their luxurious fur. Elk, brown bears, deer, wolves, lynx, foxes, marten, and muskrats also make their homes in the taiga.

Continuing south of the taiga region is a belt of gently rolling grassland called the steppe. The openness of the steppe has influenced the

types of animals that live there. These animals include burrowers, such as marmots, as well as mouse species. Farther south are skunks, foxes, wolves, and antelope. Bird species include bustards, eagles, kestrels, and larks. Approximately 200 species of birds reside along the Volga River delta. They share the region with wild boars and approximately 30 other mammals.[3]

In the Caucasus Mountains, a mountain goat called the tur makes its home. Bezoar goats also live in these mountains, along with mouflons, chamois, brown bears, and the European bison. Birds of the region include imperial eagles, peregrine falcons, goshawks, and snowcocks.

The Kamchatka Peninsula has salmon, brown bears, sea otters, seals, and more than 200 species of birds, including auks, tufted puffins, and swans. Ussuriland's warm climate nurtures animals that exist nowhere else in Russia, such as the Asian black bear, the Siberian tiger, and the rare Amur leopard.

SIBERIAN TIGER

The Siberian, or Amur, tiger is the largest tiger in the world. Siberian tigers can weigh more than 600 pounds (272 kg) and grow up to 10.75 feet (3.3 m) in length. They live in the birch forests of eastern Russia where there are few people. Even so, the Siberian tiger is endangered because of hunting and habitat loss. Only 400 to 500 of these tigers still survive in the wild, but their population appears to be stable.[4]

Wild goats including the tur live in the mountainous regions of Russia.

PLANTS

The permafrost of the tundra doesn't allow many plants to survive. However, a fragile layer of lichens grows there, as well as mosses, grasses, and flowers. Farther south are trees such as the dwarf Arctic birch.

Russia's taiga is the largest forest of this type in the world.[5] Its coniferous forest includes evergreens such as spruces, firs, and larches. Mosses, grasses, lichens, berries, and mushrooms find the shady forest floor hospitable. At the southern end of the taiga are deciduous trees. These are trees that shed their leaves in fall and include oak, ash, aspen, birch, elm, and maple.

Grassland defines the steppe region. Many species of grasses sway in the breezes that sweep this open land. Mosses, lichens, and wildflowers also grow here. However, grain cultivation has replaced much of the natural vegetation due to the area's rich soil.

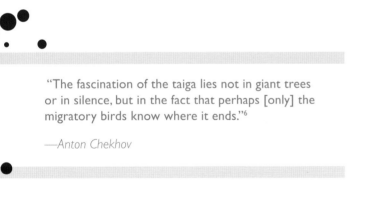

"The fascination of the taiga lies not in giant trees or in silence, but in the fact that perhaps [only] the migratory birds know where it ends."[6]

—Anton Chekhov

The dense evergreen forests of Russia's taiga region

The Volga River delta, where the river empties into the Caspian Sea, boasts a wide variety of plants, including pink and white Caspian lotus flowers. In the Caucasus Mountains, more than 6,400 different tree, plant, and wildflower species grow.[7] Some of the trees found there include oak, birch, and date plum. Flowering plants include rhododendron and epigea, a small shrub.

In the Kamchatka Peninsula, volcanic activity produces minerals that fertilize the soil. Poplar, aspen, alder, and willow trees as well as subalpine shrubs flourish there. In the south, the lush monsoon forest of Ussuriland is full of exotic plants. Vegetation includes Manchurian walnut and Amur cork trees, ginseng plants, wild grapes, and lianas, a type of climbing vine.

ENVIRONMENTAL THREATS

Russia's environmental problems include pollution, soil erosion, and deforestation. In 2007, it was estimated that 69 percent of Russian cities experience significant air pollution from vehicles and coal-fired power plants.[8] Saint Petersburg and Moscow have pollution levels well beyond national limits. Russia has been working toward reducing air pollution, and its emissions of greenhouse gases have been falling since 1990. In 2004, Russia also ratified the Kyoto Protocol, which calls for countries to limit the amount of greenhouse gases they emit.

Throughout Russia, drinking water becomes polluted when rust and chlorine seep from old water pipes. In addition, the Volga, Don, Kama, Kuban, and Oka Rivers experience pollution from viruses and bacteria. In some cases, the levels of contaminants are 100 times the allowable limit.[9] The Volga in particular experiences pollution from industrial waste, agricultural runoff, and sewage. Lake Baikal is the subject of an ongoing debate between scientists and the Russian government about stopping the pollution caused by dumping industrial waste on the lakeshore.

BAIKAL SEAL

Baikal seals live in Lake Baikal in Siberia. They are the smallest type of seal and the only ones that live in freshwater their entire lives. In the spring, the females make dens out of ice and then give birth to one or two pups at a time. More than 60,000 seals are estimated to live in Lake Baikal, but water pollution might be affecting their health.[11]

Russia's vast oil and natural gas reserves also cause pollution problems. In Chechnya, a pipeline has leaked approximately 30 million barrels of oil into the ground.[10] Near the Ob River, oil spills have contaminated the water. Oil and gas pipelines on the tundra have affected reindeer migration routes. And the heat from gas mining has melted the permafrost on the Yamal Peninsula, causing land to erode into the sea.

Radioactive contamination comes from nuclear accidents and testing. In 1986, the Chernobyl nuclear power plant had a severe accident in Ukraine, then part of the Soviet Union. Approximately 2 million Russians are still suffering from cancer and heart problems due to the lingering radioactivity.[12] A similar problem exists in Chelyabinsk from a 1957 nuclear accident. Because of this, in 1991, the Worldwatch Institute declared nearby Lake Karachay the most polluted spot on Earth.[13]

The grand forests of the taiga are being cleared out at a rate of approximately 9.9 million acres (4 million ha) a year.[14] Near the Caspian Sea and in the Kalmyk steppe, the overgrazing of sheep is causing desertification of the land. This is when the land gradually turns into a desert due to loss of vegetation.

But all is not lost. Russia is trying to preserve its flora and fauna, especially the habitats of endangered species. It currently has approximately 100 nature preserves, 35 national parks, 70 special-purpose reserves (spaces protected during specific seasons), and other nature parks.[15]

WRANGEL ISLAND RESERVE

In the frigid waters of the Arctic sit the Wrangel and Herald Islands. Established in 1976 as a protected reserve, these islands boast the highest level of biodiversity in the high Arctic. They are home to the world's largest population of Pacific walrus, a high density of polar bear dens, and the only place in Asia where the snow goose lives. The islands are also a major feeding ground for the gray whale and home to reindeer. In addition, approximately 100 migratory birds make their way to the islands every year, including the endangered peregrine falcon.[16]

Russians are working to protect their endangered wildlife, including the nearly extinct Amur leopard.

CHAPTER 4
HISTORY: HOME OF THE TSARS

Primitive humans lived in Russia before the most recent Ice Age, approximately 20,000 to 26,000 years ago. When the Ice Age began, they disappeared, as did humans throughout most of Europe, perhaps moving south to a warmer climate.

Scientists believe as Earth warmed up approximately 10,000 to 16,000 years ago, people migrated back to Russia from Ukraine and settled along the Black Sea coast. In 1000 BCE, a group of nomads called the Cimmerians settled the region, followed by several more groups.

In the late 700s and early 800s, Germanic people explored the Volga River region and started trading amber, honey, wax, furs, and timber. Merchants from Iran and North Africa also came in search of these goods. Khazars, Turkic merchants from the northern Caucasus

Siberia's frigid climate preserves remnants of the last Ice Age, including the bodies of woolly mammoths, which early Russians likely hunted.

KHAZARS

Russian Jews might be able to trace their ancestry back to a Turkic-speaking tribe called the Khazars. In the mid-700s, the Khazars controlled an empire in the northern Caucasus region. They were a sedentary people who grew gardens and vineyards. Ruled by a semireligious leader called a *khagan* and tribal chieftains known as *begs*, they decided to adopt the Jewish religion. This decision makes the Khazars unique in the history of this region.

region, took advantage of these trading activities and established a commercial empire in southeast Russia along the Volga River.

In the meantime, Scandinavian traders had established trading centers at Lake Ladoga and Lake Onega in northern Russia. By 830, they had moved to the central-eastern part of Russia, and it is during the mid-ninth century that the first mention of the state of "Rus" appeared in written documents. The first ruler of the Rus dynasty was a Scandinavian named Rurik, who became the leader of Novgorod around 862. His descendants, the princes of Novgorod, raided areas as far south as Baghdad in Iraq and Constantinople (now Istanbul) in Turkey. Prince Oleg, Rurik's kinsman, captured the entire Dnieper River all the way from the Black Sea to the Ukrainian city of Kiev. In 882, Prince Oleg moved the seat of power to Kiev and began ruling the Kievan Rus' kingdom.

KIEVAN RUS'

Kievan Rus' had a unique system of government called the rota system. Each male member of the House of Rurik was entitled to a share of land in Kiev. The oldest member of the family became the grand prince of Kiev, while the younger members became junior princes. The grand prince was the supreme protector over all of Kiev. He assigned provinces to the junior princes, where they would each rule on a throne. He also settled disputes between them. When the grand prince died, the provinces were redistributed among the junior princes.

A monument to Prince Vladimir, who brought Christianity to Russia, in Kiev, Ukraine

Between the late tenth and early twelfth centuries, the princes of Kiev wanted to make Russia a world power; however, the country's religion isolated it from the rest of the world. Most Russians were pagans, while other areas of the world practiced Judaism, Islam, or Christianity.

In 988, Prince Vladimir chose the Christian religion of Greek Orthodox. He forced people to become baptized, destroyed pagan artifacts, and built numerous Christian churches. This move helped the world perceive Kievan Rus' as a civilized state.

After Vladimir's death in 1015, Kievan Rus' continued to develop for more than 200 years. At its height, it had approximately 300 cities and a population of 7 to 8 million people.[1]

Despite its successes, Kievan Rus' suffered from political instability. When a grand prince died, junior princes fought over succession. Sometimes many years passed before a new successor was chosen. Additionally, principalities concentrated on their own interests rather than the interests of Kievan Rus' as a whole.

From 1139 to 1237, rivalries between princes grew worse, and Kievan Rus' became fractured. When the Mongols, or Tatars, invaded first in 1223 and later in 1237, the principalities were too independent to work together to address this new threat.

Russia is named after the ancient Rus people.

TATAR RULE

Under the command of Batu, nephew of the Great Khan who ruled the Tatars, 120,000 Tatar soldiers marched into eastern Russia and Europe.[2] By 1240, they had captured Moscow, destroyed the city of Vladimir, and taken Kiev.

The Tatars set up a system that allowed the Kievan princes to retain most of their power. Even so, the Tatars' impact was profound. When they conquered Russia, they destroyed several cities and killed approximately 10 percent of the population between 1237 and 1240.[3] The Russian economy didn't recover until the mid-fourteenth century. In addition, the rota system disappeared and was replaced by the appanage system, under which each province became a separate and permanent property of a prince. Finally, Kiev lost its place as the center of Russian power.

The western part of the Tatar empire was called the Golden Horde.

THE MUSCOVY ERA

During the fourteenth and fifteenth centuries, Moscow rose as a seat of power in Russia. This is called the Muscovite period of Russian history. Established as a principality in 1263, Moscow was ideally situated near several rivers and along the resulting trade routes. Plus, the center of the Orthodox Church had moved from Kiev to Moscow. By 1350, Moscow had become powerful enough to stand up to Tatar rule, and in 1380, Grand Prince Dmitry Donskoy was able to unify the other princes and defeat the Tatar army in battle. Even though the Tatars retook control of Moscow a couple years later, their power was greatly diminished. By 1480, they had completely left the region.

From 1462 to 1505, Ivan the Great ruled. He was the first leader to occasionally use the title of tsar. Because much of Muscovy was

OPRICHNIKI

In 1564, Ivan the Terrible was determined to find traitorous boyars in his realm. To do this, he created a new security force called the *oprichniki*, or "blackness of hell." These men wore black clothing, rode black horses, and carried brooms to symbolize they were sweeping traitors from the land. For seven years, the oprichniki arrested, tortured, and killed thousands of nobility and clergy, as well as their families and supporters. In early 1570, Ivan had them attack Novgorod because he didn't believe the citizens there had surrendered completely to his rule. Tens of thousands of people were slaughtered at this time. Two years later, Ivan's reign of terror ended when he had most of the oprichniki leaders executed.

fragmented, he worked hard to unify it under his rule. He expanded the Muscovite state and increased his own power. His son, Vasily III, did the same. He ruled from 1505 to 1533.

In 1547, Ivan the Terrible, a man known for his cruelty and unpredictable temper, ascended the throne. He was the first to be officially crowned "tsar of all Russia." Ivan established a *zemsky sobor*, or "assembly of the land." This council allowed Ivan to seek advice from representatives of the boyars, clergy, and merchant class. Ivan also strengthened the military and won two important battles to gain control of the cities of Kazan and Astrakhan. These victories expanded the Muscovite state east to the Urals and south to the Caspian Sea.

After Ivan's death in 1584, Russia entered a period of chaos known as the Time of Troubles. This period saw numerous revolts and a series

Ivan the Terrible

of pretenders who tried to take the throne, including small landholders, peasants, and three men known as the False Dmitrys. The Time of Troubles ended with the rise of the Romanov dynasty.

THE ROMANOVS

In 1613, Mikhail Romanov became the first of several weak tsars. During this time, Russian territory expanded west into Ukraine and east past the Ural Mountains. However, conditions for peasants worsened, leading to numerous revolts and uprisings.

One type of lower-class peasant was the serf, who was in many ways a slave. Serfs were the property of landlords. They couldn't travel or get married without permission, and they could be sold and separated from their families. Serfs paid rent or worked several days a week for their landlord in exchange for a plot of land.

In 1682, Peter the Great came to power. He built up the military force and created a navy to protect Russia and extend its borders to the Baltic and Caspian Seas. After spending time in western Europe, Peter brought European dress and customs into the country. He set up administrative departments to run various branches of the government, placed the church under greater governmental control, and altered the Russian calendar to more closely match the European calendar. He also moved the country's capital to Saint Petersburg in 1712 and named it after his patron saint.

A series of rulers succeeded Peter the Great, most notably German-born Catherine the Great in 1762. She was fascinated with Western philosophical ideas, particularly the Enlightenment, a movement that emphasized science and reason in studying human culture and the natural world. She also introduced European culture, including fencing and dancing, into aristocratic life. As a patron of the arts, she encouraged the development of Russian literature, music, and ballet, which began a creative period in Russia that lasted approximately 100 years. However, during her reign, conditions for Russian peasants grew even worse, and in 1775, the government put down a large peasant uprising.

CATHERINE THE GREAT

When Catherine the Great was only 14 years old, she married her second cousin, Peter III, who was heir to the Russian throne. Catherine was energetic, intelligent, and ambitious. Though not pretty, her charm won her many admirers in Russia, and the aristocracy loved her cultivated manner. Peter, however, was known for being neurotic, rebellious, and an alcoholic. When it came time for Peter to assume the throne, Catherine learned he planned to kill her. Knowing the military and court supported her, Catherine went to Saint Petersburg under their protection and had herself proclaimed empress. Eight days later, Peter was assassinated. Catherine ruled as empress for the next 34 years.

In 1812, 11 years after Alexander I became tsar, French general Napoléon I invaded the country. It was part of his conquest of Europe, and he brought hundreds of thousands of soldiers with him. When Napoléon's army arrived in Moscow, however, they found the city deserted and all its food and resources gone. Napoléon was forced to retreat during a bitterly cold winter. Because the Russians blocked a southern route, he had to use a northern route, which made conditions even worse. By the time Napoléon's army left Russia, only approximately 30,000 troops had survived the long march home.[4]

Nicholas I, Alexander's brother, took power in 1825 at a time of mass peasant revolt against the monarchy. This revolt, called the Decembrist uprising, involved mostly military veterans. Approximately 600 serf revolts occurred during Nicholas's reign.[5] In order to keep the peace, Nicholas instituted numerous harsh laws, including censorship, travel restrictions, and the suppression of revolutionary groups.

His successor, Alexander II, took control of the government in 1855. Alexander II brought about a time of reform, particularly for serfs. On February 19, 1861, serfs living on privately owned land were given their freedom. Five years later, serfs living on state-owned land were set free. In total, approximately three-quarters of the country's 74 million people could now marry whomever they pleased, buy land, and become traders.[6]

For Russian peasants, times were especially hard during the Romanov dynasty.

In 1867, the United States bought Alaska from Russia for $7.2 million.

However, this freedom came at a price. Peasants had to pay a fee to keep the land they worked. Often, they were allowed to keep only a small portion of the land they felt was theirs. They were also taxed at a higher rate than landlords. For several years after emancipation, there were even more uprisings than before.

In 1881, Alexander III came to power and worked to revoke many of the reforms instituted by his predecessor. Among his many changes, Alexander III reduced the role of peasants in government, increased censorship of the press, tried to get rid of jury trials, and reduced the number of peasants and Jews who could attend secondary schools and universities.

In 1894, the last tsar came to power: Nicholas II. One of his accomplishments was building the Trans-Siberian Railway, but numerous problems cut his reign short. These included food and fuel shortages during World War I (1914–1918), worker revolts that led to violent clashes with the government, and the people's dissatisfaction with the repressive rule of the tsars. Nicholas tried to bring about reform by instituting a parliament called the Duma, but the people wanted more reform and they wanted it quickly. On March 15, 1917, Nicholas II abdicated the throne.

A provisional government took over, consisting of leaders from middle-class liberal parties. In the capital, a powerful soviet immediately formed, followed by other soviets throughout the country. A soviet is a council of worker deputies who were elected in factories. The soviet in Saint Petersburg worked with the provisional government, and the two ruled as a dual power. However, not everyone was happy with that setup.

REVOLUTION AND COMMUNISM

On November 7 and 8, 1917, the Bolshevik political party seized control of the provisional government. Led by Vladimir Lenin, the Bolsheviks wanted a soviet government in which the workers, peasants, and soldiers had direct rule. They believed a parliamentary system excluded the working class and thus primarily served the interests of the upper class. Not everyone agreed with the Bolsheviks, and three years of civil war followed, pitting the Bolshevik Reds against the Whites. The Whites were led by former generals and admirals from the tsarist regime and had the support of Allied forces such as France and Great Britain.

After a year of fighting, the Reds moved the capital from Saint Petersburg back to Moscow in March 1918. A month later, they adopted a flag featuring a hammer and sickle to represent workers and peasants. They also renamed their party the All-Russian Communist Party. By the time the Reds won the war, several million people had died or moved out of a country now ravaged by disease, famine, and violent conflict.

The word *Bolshevik* means "one of the majority."

The Reds instituted a Socialist form of government in 1921. They believed this was a step toward the eventual goal of Communism. To Lenin, a Communist society is a classless society in which the state controls nearly everything to defend itself from dissent. In 1922, the country was renamed the Union of Soviet Socialist Republics (USSR), or the Soviet Union, and it included Russia, Ukraine, Byelorussia, Armenia, Azerbaijan, and Georgia.

The years of War Communism (1918–1920), in which the state took over businesses and forced peasants to give up their surplus grain, had been disastrous. This policy had led to starvation and a sharp decline in production. Lenin enacted a New Economic Policy in 1921. With this plan, the state returned farming, retail, and some light industry to the people. It retained control of heavy industry, transportation, banking, and foreign trade. This brought stability to the economy and allowed the Soviet Union to experience a time of vitality and creativity. During the early 1920s, literature and art blossomed in Russia.

After Lenin's death in January 1924, Joseph Stalin came to power. He established a totalitarian state, tightened economic controls, and initiated several Five-Year Plans to turn the country into a modern industrial nation. His Five-Year Plans started in 1928 and lasted until 1953. Their aim was to develop heavy industry and collectivize agriculture. Each industry had a production plan, and factories and individual workers had to meet production quotas. The quotas were often impossible, however, and people were sometimes worked to death. In the countryside, peasants had to give up their own farms and join large collectives (farms shared by all) called kolkhozy. If peasants resisted, they were forced into prison camps or killed. By 1936, almost all peasants had been collectivized. Millions of others had died from famine.

By 1939, Russia had become an industrial nation at the expense of widespread hardship and suffering. Stalin set out to eliminate anyone who might threaten his regime. He conducted purges in which millions of people were arrested by secret police, put on trial, and imprisoned or shot. No one was above suspicion, even Stalin's friends. It was a period of terror for many in the country.

GULAGS

The Gulags were a system of Soviet forced-labor camps. They existed from the 1920s through the 1950s under control of the secret police. Prisoners were expected to chop down trees or work in construction, usually in harsh conditions with little food. Some scholars believe between 15 and 30 million people died in the Gulag system before the camps were finally shut down.[9]

When Germany invaded Russia in 1941, the Soviet Union entered World War II (1939–1945). By October of that year, Germany controlled the land where approximately 30 percent of the population lived.[7] Despite these staggering losses, Stalin appealed to the people's patriotism, reorganized the army, and established relations with Great Britain and the United States. In 1942, the Russian army was able to defeat the Germans in the city of Stalingrad, now known as Volgograd, on the Volga River. It was a major turning point in the war. By the time the war ended in 1945, approximately 27 million Russians had been killed, and the city of Stalingrad had been destroyed.[8]

After World War II, the Soviet Union expanded its sphere of influence into the areas of Eastern Europe it had liberated from German control during the war. As a result, an era known as the Cold War (1945–1991) began between the Soviet Union and the United States. While there was no actual war between the two sides, there was an arms race, a space race, and competition throughout the world, keeping tensions high between the two countries.

After Stalin died in March 1953, his successor, Nikita Khrushchev, introduced measures of relaxation known as "the Thaw." He closed the prison camps known as Gulags, relaxed censorship, and hoped for better relations with the United States. However, by the 1960s, tensions were at an all-time high. The most dangerous event of that era was the Cuban Missile Crisis of

SPACE RACE

On October 4, 1957, the Soviet Union sent a small artificial satellite into space. Named Sputnik 1, or "traveler," it was the first man-made object to orbit Earth. The success of Sputnik spurred competition between the United States and the Soviet Union. In 1958, the United States launched its own satellite, and President Dwight D. Eisenhower created NASA, an agency dedicated to space exploration. The Soviets won the race to launch a person into Earth's orbit in 1961, but by the end of the decade, the United States was the first to send people to the moon.

On November 3, 1957, Russia launched the first living creature—a dog named Laika—into space aboard Sputnik 2.

October 1962, when the United States and the Soviet Union came close to nuclear war.

After Khrushchev was deposed by his own government in 1964, Leonid Brezhnev tried to take the country back to the days of Stalin in some ways. He did not reopen the Gulags, but he restricted travel, imposed stronger censorship, and tried to challenge the United States as a world power.

Mikhail Gorbachev took power in 1985. His reforms included instituting a policy of perestroika, or "rebuilding," in which factories and farms were modernized and became more productive. He also introduced the idea of glasnost, or "openness," which allowed people to speak openly against the government.

The invisible line separating the Soviet Union from western Europe was called the Iron Curtain.

By the late 1980s, Communist regimes around the world were under pressure to change. This change began in 1989 in eastern European countries such as East Germany, Poland, and Czechoslovakia, where people marched in protest against their governments. By the end of the year, most eastern European countries were free of Communist control.

Gorbachev tried to reform the Soviet Union, but his efforts were in vain. In August 1991, those who wanted to return to Stalinist practices attempted to overthrow Gorbachev. Their attempt failed. However, Gorbachev could no longer rule the entire Soviet Union.

On December 25, 1991, the Soviet Union dissolved into 15 countries, with Russia being the largest and most powerful.

MODERN RUSSIA

Boris Yeltsin was the first president of the new regime. In 1992, Yeltsin made a radical economic transition, forcing Russia to switch from its Communist system to capitalism very quickly. The result of this for most Russians was terrible. The value of Russia's currency fell. People lost all of their money because of inflation. The government even defaulted on its loans. The crisis peaked in 1998 when the economy collapsed.

In the middle of this economic crisis, Chechnya, a mostly Muslim republic in the southwestern part of Russia, tried to break away. Yeltsin refused to allow Chechnya to leave, resulting in a war that lasted more than a decade.

CHECHNYA

Chechnya and Russia share a turbulent history. In 1859, Russia conquered the primarily Muslim North Caucasus region of Chechnya after 200 years of fighting. Chechnya broke free briefly after the 1917 revolution, but the Soviet Union recaptured it. After World War II, Stalin accused the Chechens of supporting Germany, so he had them shipped to Siberia and central Asia in a mass deportation. The Chechens were allowed back home during Khrushchev's reign, but when the Soviet Union finally collapsed, they declared their independence. Years of fighting followed as Russia tried to regain control of the region. A 1996 peace agreement left Chechnya with some autonomy but not complete freedom from Russia.

Yeltsin retired on December 31, 1999. Vladimir Putin became acting president immediately and was elected in his own right in March 2000. Putin served as president until 2008, as prime minister from 2008 to 2012, and was reelected president again in 2012. Although Putin was more authoritarian than Yeltsin and free media disappeared during his time, Putin became extremely popular. He created a sense of Russian nationalism and revived the Russian economy, thanks in part to the great international demand for oil and natural gas, two of Russia's major resources. Since 2000, the economy and standard of living for Russians has been increasing every year. The government may not be as democratic as some would like, but the economic progress is welcome.

Vladimir Putin has served as both the president and prime minister of Russia.

CHAPTER 5
PEOPLE: PROUD TRADITIONS

Despite its size, Russia is only the ninth-most populous country in the world.[1] Its population density is low, especially in rural areas such as Siberia. Nearly three-fourths of Russians live in cities, and the vast majority live west of the Ural Mountains.[2]

A major challenge in Russia is that its population is declining, making it difficult for the country to maintain its industry, agriculture, and armed forces. If the current trend continues, experts predict Russia's population may drop from more than 142 million to 107 million by 2050.[3]

The reason for the decline is not just a low birthrate but also a high mortality rate due to substance abuse, poverty, and illness. The situation was much worse ten years ago, when Russia was losing approximately 1 million people a year.[4] Political stability, a higher standard of living, and

Russians in the country's sparsely populated rural north have developed skillful ways of surviving.

Population

Per Square Mile		Per Square Km
Over 2,500		Over 1,000
650 to 2,500		250 to 1,000
65 to 650		25 to 250
13 to 65		5 to 25
0 to 13		0 to 5

ARCTIC OCEAN

Chukchi Sea

Bering Strait

Gulf of Anadyr

Bering Sea

PACIFIC OCEAN

Barents Sea

East Siberian Sea

Anadyr

Baltic Sea

Kaliningrad

Lake Ladoga

White Sea

Murmansk

Kara Sea

Laptev Sea

Saint Petersburg

Arkhangel'sk

Magadan

Petropavlovsk-Kamchatskiy

Moscow

Yaroslavl'

Vorkuta

Pechora

Ob

Yenisey

Lena

Sea of Okhotsk

Tula

Oka

Nizhniy Novgorod

Dnieper

Voronezh

Kazan

Serov

Kama

Yakutsk

Black Sea

Penza

Perm'

Don

Volga

Yekaterinburg

Kolyma

Rostov-on-Don

Samara

Ufa

Lena

Dolinsk

Krasnodar

Orenburg

Chelyabinsk

Irtysh

Ob

Amur

Khabarovsk

Pyatigorsk

Astrakhan

Omsk

Krasnoyarsk

Amur

Ussuri

Caspian Sea

Novosibirsk

Barnaul

Irkutsk

Lake Baikal

Vladivostok

Sea of Japan

NORTH ↑

Population Density of Russia

improved medical care have since slowed the decline.

Another way of increasing the population is through immigration. Russia is encouraging people to immigrate to the country by providing them with jobs, housing, and financial incentives.

Mainly, though, Russia wants Russian-speaking immigrants. Other immigrants are generally not welcomed. This is because Russians are worried about their national identity being overwhelmed by outsiders, a point of view that limits the number of immigrants allowed into the country.

DEMOGRAPHICS

Total population	142,517,670
Median age	38.8 years
Male life expectancy	60.11 years
Female life expectancy	73.18 years
Population growth rate	-0.48 percent
Birth rate	10.94 births/ 1,000 population
Death rate	6.03 deaths/ 1,000 population
Gender ratio at birth	1.06 males/female[5]

ETHNIC GROUPS

Russians make up approximately 80 percent of the country's population, while more than 120 minority groups make up the other 20 percent.[6] Some ethnic minorities have fewer than 1,000 members, while others have more than 1 million. These larger minorities include Tatars, Ukrainians, Chuvash, Bashkirs, Chechens, and Armenians. Some of the smaller minorities include Komi, Udmurts, Mari, and Mordovians.

Approximately 72 percent of the Russian population is between 15 and 64 years of age.

The Tatars make up the largest minority group in Russia. These Turkic people descended from the Siberian Tatars who joined the Mongol army in the thirteenth century. They are also descended from earlier Hunnic, Turkic, and Finno-Ugric peoples who lived in the middle Volga River region. Today, Tatars practice Islam, and approximately 1.5 million live in Tatarstan in east-central Russia. Another 100,000 make their home in western Siberia.[7]

The Chuvash and Bashkirs are both Turkic peoples who live in the middle Volga region. The Chuvash are descended from pre-Mongol settlers. They practice an Orthodox Christian religion and live in the Chuvash Republic west of Tatarstan. The Bashkirs practice both Islam and Eastern Orthodox religions. Approximately half live in the Republic of Bashkortostan.[8]

The vast majority of people in the country are Russian.

ETHNIC POPULATIONS

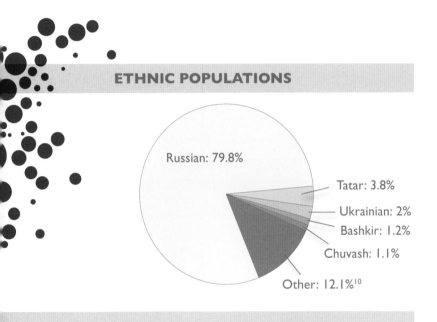

Russian: 79.8%

Tatar: 3.8%

Ukrainian: 2%

Bashkir: 1.2%

Chuvash: 1.1%

Other: 12.1%[10]

The North Caucasus region contains approximately 19 ethnic minorities. The largest of these groups, the Chechens, number approximately 1 million.[9] They live in Chechnya in southwestern Russia, practice Islam, and speak one of the Nakh languages. Having battled for independence with Russia and the Soviet Union since the 1830s, the Chechens now experience some autonomy. Other groups in the Caucasus region include the Turkic-speaking Kumyk and Nogai peoples in Dagestan and the Karachay and Balkar peoples in central Caucasus.

In central and northern European Russia live the Finno-Ugric peoples. Ancestors of Hungarians, Estonians, and Finns, they speak a Finno-Ugric language and practice a variety of religions. These peoples

A Chechen woman admires a display of headscarves, which many Muslim women wear.

include the Muslim Mordvin, approximately half of whom live in the Republic of Mordovia.[11] The Udmurts are another Finno-Ugric group who practice an Orthodox Christian religion and live mostly in Udmurtia. The Mari people practice animism, and approximately half of them live in Mari El.[12]

More than 30 ethnic minorities live in Siberia and the Far East, yet they make up only approximately 5 percent of the population there.[13] The Buryat Mongols are the largest group with a population of approximately 440,000.[14] They live north of Mongolia in Buryatia and Zabaykalsk, and they practice shamanism and Tibetan Buddhism. The Buryat are related to the Khalkha Mongols and speak a similar language. They originally lived as nomadic herders but have since converted to cattle breeding.

The Nenets number approximately 35,000 and are the largest of the groups in the north.[15] They include both nomadic reindeer herders and a

NENETS REINDEER HERDERS

In northwestern Siberia, just above the Arctic Circle, live the Nenets reindeer herders. Every year, approximately 10,000 Nenets herd hundreds of thousands of reindeer in a set migration pattern.[16] In the summer, they travel hundreds of miles north so the reindeer can feed on tundra pastureland. When the weather grows cold, they head south to spend the winter below the Arctic Circle. By the end of their harrowing journey, they have traveled approximately 680 miles (1,100 km), crossed frozen rivers, and faced temperatures as low as -58 degrees Fahrenheit (-50°C).[17]

smaller group of forest dwellers. The Nenets speak a Samoyedic language. Other ethnic minorities living in Siberia and the Far East include the Yakut (or Sakha), Tuvans, Khakass, and Altai.

THE RUSSIAN LANGUAGE

While there are dozens of minority languages in Russia, just about everyone in the country speaks Russian, an Indo-European language. This group of languages includes Germanic and Slavic languages. The Russian language shares most of its characteristics with the Slavic languages of Ukrainian and Belarusian.

Written Russian uses the Cyrillic alphabet, which is very different from the English alphabet. Only one-quarter of the Russian alphabet consists of characters used in English. The origins of the Cyrillic alphabet can be traced to the ninth century, when the missionaries Cyril and Methodius developed a written language for the Slavs to help bring Christianity to more people. Later, their alphabet was simplified into the Cyrillic alphabet and named after Cyril to honor him. Cyrillic is based on the Greek alphabet but with a few more letters.

The Cyrillic alphabet is mostly phonetic, meaning it is based on sound. Some familiar-looking letters have different sounds than in English. For instance, the Russian *B* has a "v" sound, and the *H* is pronounced as an "n."

Russian nouns are more complicated than in English because letters are placed on the end of nouns to identify their function in a sentence.

YOU SAY IT!

English	Russian
Hello	Zdrastvuytye (ZDRAHST-vooy-tyeh)
Good-bye	Da svidanya (dah svee-DAHN-yah)
Excuse me	Prastitye (prah-STEET-yeh)
Thank you	Spasiba (spah-SEE-bah)

Verbs, however, are simpler. They have fewer tenses than in English. For instance, there is no present-tense form of the verb *to be*. Additionally, Russians don't use articles such as *a* or *the*. For example, the sentence "This is a book" in English would be *Eto Kniga* in Russian, which translates to "This book."

RELIGION

In 988, Prince Vladimir changed Kievan Rus' from a country that followed many gods to one that followed the Russian Orthodox religion. For the next 1,000 years, Russian Orthodoxy had an exalted status as the national religion of Russia. In fact, when Constantinople fell in 1453, Russia viewed itself as the center of Christianity.

After the formation of the Soviet Union, the government didn't want anything else competing with people's loyalty, so it encouraged Russians to become atheists. A limited number of churches were still allowed, but a great many were seized or destroyed.

After the decline of Communism in 1991, many Russians wanted to go back to their Russian Orthodox roots. Churches were rebuilt, and they could also start new dioceses and build monasteries. Today, 15 to 20 percent of Russians consider themselves practicing members of the Russian Orthodox church.[18] There may be many more who do not practice the religion yet still consider themselves Russian Orthodox.

Russian Orthodoxy is closely related to Roman Catholicism, except members of this faith do not follow the Pope. Their leader is the patriarch of Moscow and all Russia, and he resides in Saint Daniel Monastery in Moscow. Members of the Russian Orthodox church stand for services and bend their heads or bow to pray, sometimes touching their foreheads and palms on the floor. Clergy are allowed to marry, and crosses have three bars instead of just one.

In addition to Russian Orthodoxy, Russians practice several other forms of Christianity, and these groups form approximately 2 percent of the population.[19] They include Baptists, Seventh Day Adventists, Evangelicals, Old Believers (Russian Orthodox people who broke away from the church), and Unified Evangelical Lutherans.

Muslims are the second-largest religious group in Russia, and they make up 10 to 15 percent of the population.[20] Muslims are followers of Islam, a religion based on the belief that the word of God, or Allah, was revealed to the Prophet Muhammad. In Russia, this religion is practiced mainly in the Caucasus region near the Volga River and in Siberia. Many Tatars are Muslims.

Jewish people also live in Russia. Unfortunately, their history is one of discrimination and repression. Starting in 1881, when Jews were unfairly blamed for assassinating Tsar Alexander II, angry mobs attacked Jews in riots called pogroms, destroying their property and injuring or killing them. Pogroms took place in more than 200 cities or towns that year.[21] After this initial period of violence, pogroms still occurred intermittently into the twentieth century. When Gorbachev instituted his policy of openness, many Jews were granted permission to emigrate to Israel and other countries. Currently, approximately one-tenth of Russia's Jewish population resides in Moscow.[22]

Some ethnic minorities, such as the Yakut people of eastern Siberia, practice shamanism. In shamanism, it is believed healers, or shamans, have supernatural power.

Ribbons tied to poles mark Lake Baikal, a holy site for the area's indigenous shamans.

CHAPTER 6
CULTURE: CELEBRATED ARTS

What does it mean to be Russian? Russians have been asking themselves this question for centuries. It is in part this question that drove Russian writers, composers, dancers, and artists to produce some of the greatest works the world has ever known, particularly in literature and music.

LITERATURE

The golden age of Russian literature began in 1820 with Alexander Pushkin and lasted until 1880. Russians regard Pushkin as their greatest writer, a poet as important to Russian literature as playwright William Shakespeare is to English literature. Pushkin wrote short poems, plays, stories, and long verse.

Dancers in the Royal Russian Ballet perform *Swan Lake*. Ballet is just one of the many art forms Russia is known for.

Other famous authors followed Pushkin in the golden age, including Mikhail Lermontov, Nikolai Gogol, Ivan Turgenev, and Fyodor Dostoyevsky. Many consider Dostoyevsky to have had the greatest influence on twentieth-century writers. In his writing, he explored people's inner natures—their flaws and strengths. His four greatest novels are *Crime and Punishment* (1866), *The Idiot* (1868), *The Possessed* (1872), and *The Brothers Karamazov* (1880).

> *The Brothers Karamazov* was the last novel Dostoyevsky wrote.

Leo Tolstoy also wrote during the golden age. Often considered the finest novelist in world literature, he is best known for the novels *War and Peace* (1869) and *Anna Karenina* (1877). The first is about Napoléon's invasion of Russia, and the second is a tragic love story about a woman involved with an army officer.

Anton Chekhov was part of the silver age of Russian literature, which ran from 1890 until 1917. He became famous for exploring the lives of ordinary people, and from 1888 until his death in 1904, he wrote more than 50 short stories addressing that theme. He also composed four well-known plays: *The Seagull* (1895), *Uncle Vanya* (1897), *Three Sisters* (1901), and *The Cherry Orchard* (1904).

In the 1930s, Stalin instituted a policy of socialist realism that dictated subject matter, style, and political viewpoints. If writers rebelled,

Famous Russian author Leo Tolstoy converses with his grandchildren.

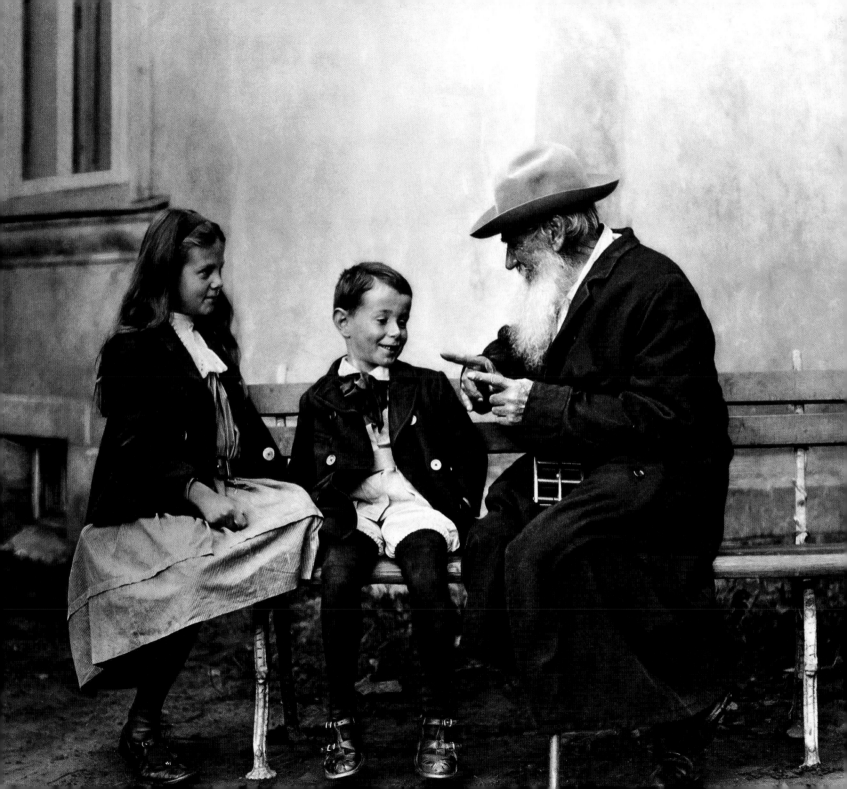

they faced prison camps or death. After Stalin died, writers were given more freedom. However, some of them still struggled to get their work published in Russia. Boris Pasternak was able to get his novel *Doctor Zhivago* (1957) published only in Western countries. Friends of Pasternak smuggled the manuscript out to Europe, where it was published the first time. It won the Nobel Prize for Literature, but Pasternak was not allowed to leave the country to receive the award.

With Gorbachev in power in 1985, novels that had previously been published only in other countries could finally be printed in Russia. As Russia emerged from Communism, new writers rose to prominence, including many women. For example, Ludmilla Petrushevskaya wrote *The Time—Night* (1992), a novel about a woman living in poverty who takes care of her troubled family. Tatyana Tolstaya wrote two imaginative volumes of short stories: *On the Golden Porch* (1990) and *Sleepwalker in a Fog* (1993).

Baba-Yaga is said to live in a hut that stands on birds' legs.

In addition to literature, Russia has a long tradition of folktales called *skazki*. During the golden age, both writers and composers drew on them for inspiration. "Ivan, the Firebird, and the Gray Wolf" and "Vasilisa" are well-known skazki that include magic, talking animals, and dolls that come to life. Baba-Yaga is a famous ogress from Russian folklore who steals her victims and eats them.

A folk musician playing a traditional Russian gusli

MUSIC

Folk music has existed in Russia for hundreds of years. Peasants often sang calendar songs, which were tied to the growing season. They sang about the harvest, prison, love, and other life events. Often they used folk instruments unique to Russia, such as a balalaika, a triangular guitar; a *gusli,* a stringed instrument; and a *garmon* or *bayan,* two types of accordions.

The 1800s ushered in a musical golden age in tandem with literature's golden age. The first composer was Mikhail Glinka, who wrote from 1836 to 1855 and was the father of Russian classical music. In his compositions, he combined Russian folk music, religious music, and Russian folktales to create a distinctly Russian sound.

In 1861 and 1862, composer Mily Balakirev formed a group called the Five. Besides Balakirev, it included composers César Cui, Modest Mussorgsky, Nikolai Rimsky-Korsakov, and Alexandr Borodin. Similar to Glinka, members of the Five borrowed heavily from traditional Russian music and became known for promoting Russian nationalism. They also aligned themselves with other modern European composers, such as Chopin and Liszt. The song "Flight of the Bumblebee" from Korsakov's opera *The Tale of Tsar Saltan* (1899–1900) is one of the most well-known pieces from the group.

Pyotr Ilich Tchaikovsky is the most famous of Russia's composers. Breaking away from the Five's politics and philosophy, his music had beautiful melodies and encompassed a variety of styles. He wrote 11 operas and three famous ballets: *Swan Lake* (1876), *Sleeping Beauty* (1889), and *The Nutcracker* (1892). He also wrote an orchestral piece called the *1812 Overture* (1880), which is about Russia's battle with Napoléon and features real canons.

A scene from *The Nutcracker*, a ballet by Russian composer Tchaikovsky

In the twentieth century, Sergey Rachmaninoff and Igor Stravinsky rose to prominence. Rachmaninoff became one of Russia's greatest pianists while Stravinsky is considered the greatest composer of the twentieth century.

During the Communist regime, Sergey Prokofiev and Dmitry Shostakovich became known as the best Soviet composers. This was quite an accomplishment because innovation and experimentation were discouraged. Perhaps the most famous composition from this time is Prokofiev's *Peter and the Wolf* (1936).

Today, classical music in Russia continues to live up to the high standard set during the golden age. But rock and pop music have become popular. Both used to be imports from Western countries, but now native Russians are recording their own unique sounds. Pop singer Alla Pugacheva is extremely popular in Russia. Known for her electrifying performances, she won numerous awards and sold more than 100 million records in the 1990s and 2000s.[1]

DANCE

Russian folk dance brings to mind men crouching down with their arms folded and kicking their legs. This form of dance goes back

Russian folk music and dance are still celebrated in the country.

many centuries, but it never reached the worldwide prominence of Russian ballet.

Ballet in Russia combined Russian folk dancing with French and Italian styles of ballet. It became known for its elaborate sets, well-trained dancers, and complex characters.

Saint Petersburg's Imperial Ballet School (now the Vaganova Academy of Russian Ballet) was the prestigious academy where the best dancers were trained. In 1838, Marius Petipa came to Saint Petersburg from France. For approximately 60 years, he worked there developing the Russian style of ballet and elevated it to an art form that gained worldwide attention and is still praised today.

Famous ballet dancers to come from Russia include Anna Pavlova (1881–1931), who toured around the world, and Vaslav Nijinsky (1890–1950), who was known for his amazing leaps. Ballet is still important to Russian culture; however, financial problems and competing

ANNA PAVLOVA

After seeing a performance of *Swan Lake,* eight-year-old Anna Pavlova knew she wanted to dance. Two years later, she entered the prestigious Imperial Ballet School in Saint Petersburg. When she graduated in 1899 at the age of 18, she was far more accomplished than most beginning ballerinas. In 1905, she performed the lead solo in *The Dying Swan,* wowing audiences with her expressive face and delicate performance. It became her signature role. In 1911, she formed her own company and toured the world for another 20 years.

entertainment are making it more difficult for ballet companies to attract
audiences as they once did.

ARTS AND CRAFTS

Much Russian folk art is made of wood from the country's dense forests.
Many household objects are covered in intricate carvings. Khokhloma, a
special process of painting a wooden object, was named after the town

FABERGÉ EGGS

Peter Carl Fabergé got his start when Tsar Alexander III asked him to design a fancy Easter egg for his wife, the empress. Fabergé wanted to create something better than the jeweled eggs popular in Europe, so he made an egg out of gold and painted it in white enamel. When the empress opened the eggshell, she found a gold yolk inside along with a tiny golden hen wearing a gold crown. Delighted, the tsar and his family ordered more eggs. Soon, the eggs became famous all over the world. Fabergé and his team made more than 1,000 of these works of art.[2]

in which the craft was developed. The process involves coating the object with clay and then baking it in the oven. Powdered metal is painted over the surface in black, red, and green. After a coating of varnish is applied, the object is baked again. The result is a spectacularly glossy finish with rich, deep colors that seem to glow.

Toys are another common form of Russian folk art. Made of unpainted wood, one type of toy is carved into tiny people or animals and designed to perform elaborate tricks. For instance, a toy bird will bob its head when a peg mounted on its base is pulled. Another type of toy, the *matryoshka*, is a set of nesting dolls.

Other types of folk art include niello, a type of engraved silver; brightly colored Dymkovo figurines made of clay; hand-painted lacquer boxes; and enameled and jeweled objects, such as Fabergé eggs.

Russian fine art is not as well known as the country's folk art. Russian painters in the nineteenth century did not want to experiment with form and color as their French contemporaries did. Called the Itinerants, they preferred to use their art to comment on social issues.

At the turn of the century, painters' attention turned to art for art's sake, leading to an avant-garde period of Russian painting. One of the most famous Russian artists from this time is Marc Chagall (1887–1985), who is known for his fanciful paintings.

From the late 1920s to the mid-1980s, the Soviet Union squashed artistic innovation. Propaganda rose to an art form during this period, as posters and films focused on supporting the nation's leaders and advertising Communist values. After the Soviet Union dissolved in 1991, many forms of art emerged, including painting, photography, and digital art.

Chagall designed sets and costumes for several plays and ballets, including Stravinsky's *The Firebird*.

FILM AND TELEVISION

When television first hit Soviet airwaves, it was dominated by Communist propaganda along with filmed concerts, plays, and poorly made horror movies. Under Gorbachev, television was instrumental in speeding the takedown of the Soviet Union. Gorbachev allowed more programming on Russian television—even programs that were critical of the regime. His glasnost idea exposed facts about Soviet history that had never been known to most Russians, including Stalin's atrocities. It looked as though television might become free of government control, but that was not to be. Today, there are a few independent networks, but most are still owned by the government. Even so, the range of programming available today is much broader than it was during Soviet times.

Film enjoyed more freedom than television. Early Russian films from the 1920s showed a lot of innovation. Filmmaker Lev Kuleshov popularized an editing process called montage in which separate pieces of film are spliced together to create a cohesive story. Lenin even used film to help spread his revolutionary message.

During the Soviet Union, film had to follow the socialist realism policy. After the fall of Communism, film struggled because of lack of financing. Even so, the 1994 film *Burnt by the Sun* won the Academy Award for Best Foreign-Language Film.

ARCHITECTURE

Russian Orthodox churches display a uniquely Russian form of architecture. Influenced by the designs in Byzantium and Kiev, medieval churches were boxy affairs with one or more domes. Initially, domes were shaped like helmets, but then the classic onion shape became popular. These distinctive domes can be seen all over Russia. The Cathedral of Saint Basil the Blessed in Moscow is the most famous church of this style. In Saint Petersburg, the churches are more Western than those in Moscow. They have classical columns and one central dome.

Modern architecture in Russia was realized by Fyodor Shekhtel, who drew inspiration from American architect Frank Lloyd Wright. Shekhtel designed the well-known Ryabushinsky house with a flat roof and art nouveau metalwork on the windows and front fence.

THE CATHEDRAL OF SAINT BASIL THE BLESSED

In the sixteenth century, Ivan the Terrible commissioned the Cathedral of Saint Basil the Blessed to celebrate his capture of the Mongolian city of Kazan. Legend says when Ivan the Terrible saw the completed cathedral with its colorful onion-shaped domes, he had the architect blinded so he could never create something so beautiful again.

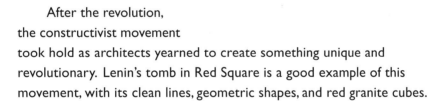

After the revolution, the constructivist movement took hold as architects yearned to create something unique and revolutionary. Lenin's tomb in Red Square is a good example of this movement, with its clean lines, geometric shapes, and red granite cubes.

During the Communist years, city planning, similar to other art forms, bowed to the demands of the state government, leaving little room for experimentation or creativity. During this period, buildings were meant to glorify the Soviet regime. Many of the beautiful and historic churches were destroyed, though some were preserved as museums.

After Stalin's death in 1953, the Soviet Union built inexpensive apartments for people in the larger cities. These units had small spaces, and dwellers often had to share a bath and kitchen. Apartments are still popular in the cities, but renters no longer have to share.

Red Square decorated for winter holidays

HOLIDAYS AND FESTIVALS

The first holiday of the year is New Year's Day. Because Christmas
celebrations were outlawed during Soviet rule, many of those traditions

were transferred to New Year's. Russians buy a New Year's tree called a *yolka*, decorate it with ornaments, and buy presents to put under it. Instead of Santa Claus, Russian children look forward to getting presents from Father Frost and the Snow Maiden.

Christmas is quieter than New Year's and is celebrated on January 7. On Christmas Eve, families eat a traditional dish called *kutya*, which is a soup with poppy seeds, honey, nuts, and barley. A church service follows at midnight.

Easter is the biggest holiday for the Russian Orthodox Church, and it occurs in spring. A church service begins at midnight on the Saturday before Easter and lasts until 4:00 a.m. The next day, families visit relatives. They bring Easter cakes called *pashkas* and decorated eggs.

Other holidays include Defender of the Motherland Day on February 23, Women's Day on March 8, May Day on May 1–2, Victory Day on May 9, Russia Day on June 12, National Unity Day on November 4, and Constitution Day on December 12.

FOOD

Traditional Russian food developed in response to Russia's long winters. To store food for this harsh season, cooks pickled or preserved berries, mushrooms, and cabbages and used them in pies and soups.

Over the centuries, Russian cuisine was also influenced by people from other lands, who introduced Russians to buckwheat, tea, spices,

VODKA

Vodka comes from the word *vada*, or "water." It is an alcoholic beverage, made from fermented grain and then filtered. The best vodka is filtered through charcoal made from birch bark. In Russia, adults drink vodka straight without sipping. Once a bottle is opened, it must be finished.

noodles, and potatoes. In turn, Russia gave the world vodka and caviar.

A typical Russian meal begins with an appetizer called *zakuski*, such as caviar or pickled herring, plus Russian bread with butter. After one or more appetizers, the main dish is served. This is often a type of soup, such as borscht, or *pelmeni*, meat-filled dumplings served with butter or vinegar. Other main courses include fish dishes, chicken Kiev, or beef Stroganoff. A typical dessert is vanilla ice cream with jam. Blini, or thin pancakes served with a variety of fillings, are a Russian favorite. They are traditionally prepared for the weeklong Russian holiday of Maslenitsa. Tea is one of the most popular beverages in Russia. Its warmth is especially welcome during the country's long winters.

SPORTS

Since the formation of the Soviet Union, Russia has become known for its dominance in the Olympic Games. The Soviet Union had so many world-class athletes that it often collected more medals than any other country. Some of its best events were gymnastics, figure skating, volleyball, basketball, track and field, weight lifting, wrestling, and boxing. Russia still produces many medal winners and usually comes just after the United States, China, and the United Kingdom in the medal count. Russia has also been chosen to host the 2014 Winter Olympics in the city of Sochi.

Russian athlete Anna Chicherova was ecstatic to win gold in the women's high jump in 2012.

Russians love soccer, or football, as they call it. There are three professional men's divisions, and Russia was chosen to host the 2018 World Cup finals. Ice hockey, fishing, and many other sports are also popular in Russia. Chess is a popular board game, and there are chess clubs throughout the country.

CHAPTER 7

POLITICS: FROM COMMUNISM TO DEMOCRACY

Russia is a federation, a union of partially self-governing regions united by a central government. It is also a democracy with national elections. As set up by its 1993 constitution, Russia has an executive, a legislative, and a judicial branch. The executive branch has the most power.

EXECUTIVE BRANCH

The president is head of the executive branch and is elected by popular vote to a maximum of two consecutive six-year terms. As head of state, the president can draft legislation and send it to the parliament, Russia's legislative body, for approval. In turn, the president can veto legislation the parliament passes. He or she can also issue decrees without approval.

Prime Minister Dmitry Medvedev was head of the Russian government in 2012.

As commander-in-chief, the president can declare war, martial law, or a state of emergency. In addition, the president nominates the head of government—the prime minister—as well as key judges and cabinet members. Russia has no vice president. If the president dies or cannot serve any longer, the prime minister is put in charge until a new president can be elected.

The prime minister is a Russian citizen appointed by the president and approved by the lower house of parliament. In addition to running the government, the prime minister also represents Russia in other countries and keeps the president informed about the government's work.

Vladimir Putin began his third term as Russia's president on May 7, 2012. Dmitry Medvedev became the country's prime minister on May 8, 2012.

LEGISLATIVE BRANCH

The legislative branch of Russia's government is a bicameral parliament called

PUTIN

Vladimir Putin was born on October 7, 1952, to a working-class family. Growing up, he loved watching spy movies, so it is no surprise he worked for the KGB, Russia's Committee for State Security, for approximately 15 years. In 1990, he retired from the KGB and worked in Saint Petersburg's mayor's office. In 1998, President Yeltsin asked him to head the Federal Security Service, Moscow's domestic antiterrorism office. A year later, Yeltsin appointed Putin as prime minister, and when Yeltsin retired on December 31, 1999, Putin became acting president. Putin won the following election with more than 50 percent of the votes.[1]

the Federal Assembly. The upper house is the Federation Council, and the lower house is the State Duma.

With two people representing each of the 83 regions, the Federation Council has 166 members. Each is appointed by regional governments to serve a four-year term.

The State Duma has 450 seats, and each member serves a four-year term. Half of State Duma representatives are elected by popular vote and apportioned according to which party received the most votes. Only parties with 7 percent or more of the popular vote can have members in the State Duma. The other half of State Duma representatives are elected in regional district elections.

The main job of the Duma is to draft legislation and send it to the Federation Council. The Federation Council votes on the legislation and usually approves it. In addition, the Duma can change the constitution or override a presidential veto with a two-thirds vote. The Federation Council approves all judicial appointments made by the president.

JUDICIAL BRANCH

Russia's judicial branch includes the Constitutional Court, the Supreme Court, and the Supreme Arbitration Court. Judges for all three courts are appointed by the president's office, and they serve for their lifetime.

The Constitutional Court has 19 members and primarily resolves disagreements between the legislative and executive branches and between the central and regional governments. It also examines constitutional rights and hears some appeals.

The Supreme Court has 23 members and rules on civil, criminal, and administrative issues. It is also the final place for an appeal to be heard after a local, district, or regional court weighs in. The Supreme Arbitration Court has 53 judges and settles disagreements in commercial matters, as well as cases other arbitration courts have already examined.

STRUCTURE OF THE GOVERNMENT OF RUSSIA

Executive Branch	Legislative Branch	Judicial Branch
President Prime Minister	Federation Council (Upper House) State Duma (Lower House)	Constitutional Court Supreme Court Supreme Arbitration Court

LOCAL GOVERNMENT

The eight federal districts are run by presidential envoys who have been appointed by the president. They coordinate communication between the president and the 83 administrative regions. They also have the authority to override regional administrations.

The 83 administrative regions are run by governors. These leaders are nominated by the president and approved by local legislatures. Smaller communities have local councils and city administrators, who are appointed by the regional governor.

Opposition parties staged a protest rally on May 1, 2012, in Vladimir, Russia.

POLITICAL PARTIES

Russia has seven registered political parties, the largest of which is United Russia, with more than 2 million members.[2] Headed by Vladimir Putin and Dmitry Medvedev, United Russia's main goal is to modernize and reform the Russian economy. The main opposition party to United Russia is the Communist Party of the Russian Federation, with more than 500,000 members.[3] It wants to nationalize some sectors of the economy and provide free distribution of land for agriculture. The second-largest opposition party is the Liberal Democratic Party, with approximately 185,000 members.[4] It believes the country has made mistakes by trying to form alliances with the West and relying too much on the free market to improve the economy. Another large political party is Just Russia, with more than 400,000 members.[5] It wants to blend socialist ideas with democratic values. Other political parties include Patriots of Russia, Right Cause, and the Yabloko Party. In 2012, the United Russia Party dominated the government. Along with Putin and Medvedev, the majority of the State Duma belonged to this party.

THE RUSSIAN FLAG

The Russian flag contains three broad horizontal stripes of equal thickness. From top to bottom, they are white, blue, and red. In 1699, Peter the Great chose this design because it resembled the Dutch flag, and he had been visiting the Netherlands at the time. Some say the colors symbolize Saint George, who was depicted on the red shield of Moscow wearing a blue cloak and mounted on a white horse. After the 1917 revolution, the flag was replaced with a gold hammer and sickle with a red star. When the Soviet Union fell, the traditional flag was reinstated on August 21, 1991.

CONSTITUTION

The most recent Russian constitution was drafted by Yeltsin's government and ratified by three-fifths of Russian voters on December 12, 1993. The constitution guarantees freedom of speech, freedom

The Russian flag

of assembly, the right to a fair trial, freedom of the press, and basic human rights. The constitution also outlines financial security for the Russian people through social security, pensions, free health care, and affordable housing.

CHALLENGES

One of Russia's biggest challenges is corruption. One corrupt practice is awarding contracts to companies to do work for Russia. State officials tell a company if it wants to be on the bidders' list, it has to pay a fee. Then the company will get the job over companies who have not paid a fee.

Electoral fraud is another corrupt practice in Russia. During the December 2011 parliamentary elections, election monitors witnessed ballot stuffing, with one person submitting multiple votes, in some polling places. Thousands protested the results, and Russian officials began an investigation. New technology was

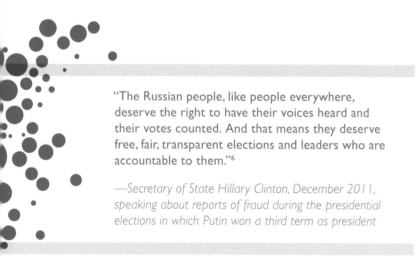

"The Russian people, like people everywhere, deserve the right to have their voices heard and their votes counted. And that means they deserve free, fair, transparent elections and leaders who are accountable to them."[6]

—*Secretary of State Hillary Clinton, December 2011, speaking about reports of fraud during the presidential elections in which Putin won a third term as president*

used during the March 2012 presidential election, including transparent ballot boxes, but the Organization for Security and Cooperation in Europe, a voting watchdog group, alleges approximately one-third of polling places in Russia still have problems with fraud.[7]

Russia also faces challenges with human rights. Russian prisoners are reportedly being tortured. In the Chechen conflict, troops are allegedly using excessive force against civilians. Police arrest and detain people who haven't broken a law. Freedom of speech is particularly hard hit. The government buys all or parts of media companies and then forces the companies to censor their content.

Transparent ballot boxes at a Moscow polling station help prevent fraud in the 2012 election.

CHAPTER 8

ECONOMICS: RICH IN RESOURCES

With the collapse of the Soviet Union in 1991, Russia moved from a planned economy to a market-based economy, but the transition wasn't easy. After price controls were removed, prices skyrocketed while Russia's currency, the ruble, fell dramatically. The economy shrunk by two-fifths and bottomed out in 1998.[1] Millions of people lost their life savings.

Government officials worked to fix the problem. They moderated tax laws and offered incentives for companies to reinvest their profits in the economy. However, government intervention and problems with corruption, weak law enforcement, and organized crime hampered foreign investment.

By the 2000s, Russia's economy was growing again, thanks in large part to its enormous oil reserves. The economy experienced a healthy

A Russian worker drills for oil, one of the country's most important natural resources.

7 percent growth rate for ten years until the world economic crisis (2008–2009) caused it to falter.[2] High oil prices helped Russia recover from that, and in 2011, it became the top oil producer in the world.[3] A middle class has emerged in Russia, and in 2011, the Russian economy was ranked seventh in the world by total gross domestic product (GDP).[4]

RUSSIA'S CURRENCY

The ruble first came into widespread circulation in 1704 during Peter the Great's reign. After the Russian revolution and subsequent civil war, runaway inflation made the ruble worthless. During the Soviet regime, a new currency called the chervonets was used until after World War II, when the ruble was restored as the national currency. Today, one ruble equals 100 kopecks. Banknotes are issued in denominations of five to 5,000 rubles and feature images from around Russia, such as the Bolshoi Theater in Moscow. Coins range from one to 50 kopecks and one to 25 rubles.

NATURAL RESOURCES

Russia has some of the largest natural gas, coal, and crude oil reserves in the world. These raw materials help drive the economy, but the market can go up and down quickly, affecting the Russian economy just as fast.

In addition, with almost half the country covered in forest, Russia is one of the leading timber exporters in the world. Unfortunately, problems with pollution, fires, insects, and wasteful timber

policies have reduced the amount and quality of wood produced. Russia is also rich in fish, diamonds, nickel, cobalt, platinum, and aluminum.

CHIEF INDUSTRIES

In the 1990s, Russia transferred most of its state-run industries to privately owned companies, with the exception of energy and defense. Approximately 37 percent of Russia's GDP comes from industry, and industry employs approximately 27.5 percent of the country's labor force.[5]

Russia's industries include mining and extraction for coal, oil, natural gas, chemicals, and metals. Russian companies are involved in all forms of machine building, including high-performance aircraft and space vehicles. Defense industries include radar, missile production, electronics, and shipbuilding. Russia makes equipment for a wide range of industries, including transportation, communication, agriculture, electric power, medicine, and science. Other manufactured products include consumer appliances, textiles, food, and handicrafts.

AGRICULTURE

Russia may have more land than any other country, but because of its cold climate, only approximately 7 percent of that land is arable.[6] The amount of land actually farmed is further reduced by overuse of chemicals, overly intensive farming, and other factors.

Agriculture accounts for 4.5 percent of Russia's GDP and employs approximately 9.8 percent of the labor force.[7] Russia's main agricultural products include grain, sugar beets, sunflower seeds, vegetables, fruits, beef, and milk.

IMPORTS AND EXPORTS

Russia has enjoyed a large trade surplus ever since the collapse of the Soviet Union. A trade surplus is when a country exports more than it imports. In 1997, Russia was admitted into the Group of Eight (G8), an

Resources of Russia

Legend:
- Cattle
- Cereal Crops
- Gas
- Iron and Steel
- Manufacturing
- Mining
- Oil
- Root Crops
- Timber

organization of countries with the largest economies. G8 countries meet at least once a year to discuss economics. In August 2012, Russia was admitted into the World Trade Organization (WTO).

In 2011, Russia imported $322.5 billion worth of products and services, making the country the eighteenth-largest importer in the world.[8] Russia's imports include electricity, oil, natural gas, machinery, vehicles, plastic, metals, food products, and pharmaceutical and medical products. Germany, China, Ukraine, and Italy are the country's primary import partners.

Russia's exports for 2011 were valued at $520.9 billion, making the country the tenth-largest exporter in the world.[9] Electricity, oil, natural gas, metals, chemicals, and wood and wood products are Russia's major exports. Export partners include Germany, the Netherlands, the United States, China, and Turkey.

INFRASTRUCTURE

Russia has 610,000 miles (982,000 km) of roads—more than all but six other countries.[10] But toward the end of the Soviet Union, the roads fell into disrepair and have only gotten worse since. Poor management, harsh climates, and the length of the roads have made it difficult to fix the problem. The government has a plan in place to build new toll roads by 2020 in addition to repairing existing roads.

With the roads in such poor shape, railroads are critical for hauling freight and passengers. Russian railroads are second only to the

United States in length and third to the United States and China in tons of freight.[11] In 2001, Russia instituted a plan to privatize the railroads. In 2012, approximately one-third of freight trains were in private hands.[12] In addition, Russia has an extensive network of city passenger trains.

Russia lost more than half its ports when the Soviet Union collapsed— its former ports are now located in other countries. This means it cannot accommodate the amount of trade entering the country by ship. With pressure from industry— particularly the oil industry—the government plans to expand and upgrade its existing ports,

ECONOMIC STATISTICS

Currency	ruble
Gross Domestic Product (GDP)	$2.414 trillion (2011 est.) world rank: 7
Per capita GDP (PPP)	$17,000 (2011 est.) world rank: 71
Population below poverty line	13.1 percent (2010 est.)
Labor force	75.41 million (2011 est.) world rank: 8
Unemployment rate	6.6 percent (2011 est.) world rank: 74
Industrial production growth rate	4.7 percent (2011 est.) world rank: 73[13]

which include Saint Petersburg, Sochi, and Vladivostok. Russia also has approximately 63,000 miles (102,000 km) of inland waterways.[14]

Russia has 1,218 airports, the fifth most in the world, but fewer than half the runways are paved.[15] Similar to Russia's other infrastructure, they need to be updated. With Russia hosting both the 2014 Winter Olympics and the 2018 World Cup soccer tournament, in 2012 plans were underway to make this happen.

TRANS-SIBERIAN RAILWAY

At almost 5,800 miles (9,300 km) in length, the Trans-Siberian Railway is the longest single-service railway in the world.[18] It winds from Moscow in the west to Vladivostok in the east, crossing the Ural Mountains and traversing vast swaths of taiga, steppe, and desert. Construction began in 1891 during Tsar Alexander III's reign, and it finally finished in 1916. Passengers who ride it today travel at a leisurely 37 miles per hour (60 km/h), giving them plenty of time to enjoy the scenery.[19]

TOURISM

From the mountains of Altai and the Komi forests to the historic Novgorod monuments and the Kazan kremlin, Russia boasts 25 World Heritage Sites. This ranks it in the top 15 countries in the world.[16] Yet it ranks only fifty-ninth out of 139 countries by number of tourists.[17]

Russia's Trans-Siberian Railway runs cross-country from Moscow to Vladivostok.

One reason for lack of tourism is that visitors must obtain a visa from the Russian Embassy to travel to Russia. The country's poor transportation, high crime rate, and language differences also make it a less desirable destination. Tourists who do visit the country primarily enjoy the cities of Moscow and Saint Petersburg.

CHALLENGES

As the Russian economy continues to grow, it faces several challenges. One of those is increasing the effort to privatize the economy. Right now, the state owns approximately 50 percent of all businesses in Russia, but the government plans to reduce its ownership.[20] The goal is to no longer control major oil companies by 2016.

Another challenge to the economy is the rise of organized crime. After the Soviet Union collapsed in 1991, criminal networks called *vory v zakone* boomed in Russia, and by the early 2000s, they numbered more than 5,000.[21] Russian organized crime groups performed money laundering (hiding the source of money obtained illegally), tax evasion, and assassinations of politicians and businesspeople. Although their activities declined in the twenty-first century, they were still a deterrent to businesses that wanted to invest in Russia.

Despite Russia's challenges, tourists still flock to Red Square and other attractions.

CHAPTER 9
RUSSIA TODAY

In the city of Moscow, Russian children are surrounded by exotic restaurants, luxurious hotels, and newly paved roads. They live in expensive 9- to 12-story apartment buildings left over from the Soviet Union. In addition to an apartment, many city-dwelling families own a small country home called a dacha for weekend getaways.

DACHAS

The Soviet government gave factories and research centers a plot of land, which the managers then divvied up for their workers. Each worker received 0.15 acres (6 ha) on which to build a dacha.[1] It was a perk for the ordinary person—a weekend retreat. It was also a way of owning land in a country where it was illegal to own anything but the items inside a state-owned home. Years later, when Gorbachev was in charge and many people were losing their jobs, dacha vegetable gardens kept Russian families fed. Today, dachas run the gamut from simple huts to fancy mansions, and Russians consider them a vital part of their culture.

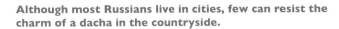

Although most Russians live in cities, few can resist the charm of a dacha in the countryside.

Russian children who grow up in the country have a very different lifestyle. Rural villages, in general, are poor. Many are emptying out as families abandon them for greater opportunities in the city. A typical village has wooden homes surrounded by enough land to grow a garden and raise a cow. Some homes do not have indoor plumbing. You can still see horse-drawn wagons making their way through villages that have few modern amenities.

One thing most Russian children have in common is how they are raised. Family is important in Russia, and parents dote on children. This love comes with strict discipline that can leave little room for self-expression or experimentation. Yet young Russians are more self-reliant and independent than ever before. Rather than having the state dictate their values, they want to decide for themselves what is right and wrong.

Approximately 15 percent of Russians are 14 years old or younger.

EDUCATION

Approximately 8 million children and teens attend school in Russia, resulting in an almost 100 percent literacy rate throughout the country.[2] Beginning at age six or seven, children are required to go to primary school, which lasts for nine years, or until students are approximately 15 years old. After primary school, the vast majority

Russian children are generally close to their families, but they also strive for independence.

of students move on to secondary school, where they study subjects including Russian language and literature, economics, history, science, art, and music.

After graduating from secondary school, students can either go on to study at a college or university, attend a vocational school, or get a job. Those who wish to attend a university must take a test. In Russia, college students become very specialized in their chosen field, so it usually takes five or six years to get a degree. Graduate degrees are not as common in Russia as they are in the United States.

EDUCATIONAL ENROLLMENT (2009)

Percent enrolled in primary school	98
Percent enrolled in secondary school	86
Percent enrolled in tertiary school	75
Number enrolled in vocational school	1.7 million[3]

FUTURE OUTLOOK

Life in Russia is very different today from how

it was in the Soviet Union. Now all Russians can own land, practice the religion of their choice, protest against the government, and buy whatever consumer goods they desire.

However, Russia faces many challenges as it moves into the twenty-first century. Its population is declining. Its natural resources are facing degradation and pollution. The economy relies too heavily on oil and natural gas. Government corruption, weak infrastructure, organized crime, slow privatization, and human rights abuses are just some of the other challenges facing the country.

LITERACY RATE

Total population	99.6 percent
Male	99.7 percent
Female	99.5 percent (2010 est.)[5]

Some might argue Russia is still in transition from a Communist country to a democracy, from a centralized economy to a market-driven economy. In April 2012, Gorbachev spoke about the future of Russia. He said, "As a transitioning country, I can say that we are a little more than halfway down the path of that transition."[4] As Russia transforms from its Soviet past into its democratic future, he asked for time and patience from the rest of the world to allow Russia to resolve its problems and complete its transition.

Victory Day on May 9 celebrates Russia's victory over Germany in World War II.

On Victory Day, Russians remember their past as they look toward the future.

[TIMELINE]

1000 BCE	The Cimmerians settle along the Black Sea in Russia.
late 700s–800s CE	The Khazars establish a commercial empire in southeast Russia.
882	Prince Oleg moves the seat of Russian power to the city of Kiev.
988	Prince Vladimir adopts the Greek Orthodox religion for the country.
1223 and 1237	After winning a battle at the river Kalka in 1223, the Tatar army leaves the country only to return in 1237 with a larger force.
1263	Moscow is established as a seat of power.
1380	Grand Prince Dmitry Donskoy leads a unified army to defeat the Tatars in battle.
1462–1505	Ivan the Great (Ivan III) rules Russia during the Muscovite period.
1547–1584	Ivan the Terrible (Ivan IV) rules Russia.
1682–1725	Peter the Great (Peter I) rules Russia during the Romanov period.
1762–1796	German-born Catherine the Great (Catherine II) rules Russia.
1812	Napoléon I invades Russia, and his army suffers many losses when it retreats during a harsh winter.

1861	On February 19, the serfs are given their freedom.
1894–1917	Nicholas II rules as the last tsar in Russian history.
1917	On November 7 and 8, the Bolsheviks seize control of the government and begin a three-year revolution.
1921	The Reds win the war and establish a Communist government.
1922	Russia is renamed as the Union of Soviet Socialist Republics.
1924	In January 1924, Vladimir Lenin dies, and Joseph Stalin comes to power.
1941	In June, Germany invades Russia during World War II. The war ends in 1945.
1953	On March 5, Joseph Stalin dies.
1953	In September, Nikita Khrushchev becomes ruler and begins to dismantle some of Stalin's repressive policies.
1985	On March 11, Mikhail Gorbachev becomes the new ruler and institutes policies of rebuilding and openness.
1991	On December 25, the Soviet Union collapses. Boris Yeltsin is the first president of Russia.
2000	In March, Vladimir Putin becomes president.

[FACTS AT YOUR FINGERTIPS]

GEOGRAPHY

Official name: Russian Federation
(in Russian, Rossiyskaya Federatisiya)

Area: 6,601,668 square miles
(17,098,242 sq km)

Climate: Ranges from steppe in the
south through humid continental in
European Russia; subarctic in Siberia
to tundra in the polar north.

Highest elevation: Mount Elbrus,
18,481 feet (5,633 m) above sea
level

Lowest elevation: Caspian Sea,
92 feet (28 m) below sea level

Significant geographic features: Ural
Mountains, Caspian Sea, Volga River,
Kamchatka Peninsula, Ussuriland

PEOPLE

Population (July 2012 est.):
142,517,670

Most populous city: Moscow

Ethnic groups: Russian, 79.8 percent;
Tatar, 3.8 percent; Ukrainian,
2 percent; Bashkir, 1.2 percent;
Chuvash, 1.1 percent; other or
unspecified, 12.1 percent

Percentage of residents living in
urban areas: 73 percent

Life expectancy: 66.46 years at birth
(world rank: 163)

Language(s): Russian, many minority
languages

Religion(s): Russian Orthodox,
15–20 percent; Muslim, 10–15
percent; other Christian, 2 percent
(estimates are of practicing
worshippers; Russia has numerous
nonbelievers and nonpracticing
believers)

GOVERNMENT AND ECONOMY

Government: federation

Capital: Moscow

Date of adoption of current constitution: December 12, 1993

Head of state: president

Head of government: prime minister

Legislature: Federal Assembly, consists of an upper house called the Federation Council and a lower house called the State Duma

Currency: ruble

Industries and natural resources: Complete range of mining and extractive industries for the natural resources of coal, oil, gas, chemicals, and metals; all forms of machine building; defense industries; road and rail transportation equipment; communications equipment; agricultural machinery, tractors, and construction equipment; electric power generating and transmitting equipment; medical and scientific

instruments; consumer durables, textiles, foodstuffs, and handicrafts. Russia also has extensive resources in wood and wood products.

NATIONAL SYMBOLS

Holidays: Russia Day, June 12

Flag: three horizontal bands of white, blue, and red (top to bottom)

National anthem: "Gimn Rossiyskoy Federatsii" (National Anthem of the Russian Federation)

National animal: brown bear

KEY PEOPLE

Prince Vladimir (980–1015), adopted Greek Orthodox as the Christian religion for Russia

Ivan the Great (1462–1505), known as the "gatherer of Russian lands," greatly expanded the Russian state

Ivan the Terrible (1533–1584), cruel ruler who was the first to give himself the title of tsar

Peter the Great (1682–1725), built up the military and created a navy as he extended Russia's borders; adopted European customs

Catherine the Great (1762–1796), known for encouraging the development of the arts and embracing Western styles of thought and culture

Nicholas II (1894–1917), last Russian tsar

Vladimir Lenin (1917–1924), first head of the Soviet state, he led the Bolsheviks in a revolution for the working class and helped transform Russia into a Communist country

Joseph Stalin (1924–1953), cruel dictator who enacted harsh economic and government controls; known for using secret police to arrest millions of people and send them to work camps

Boris Yeltsin (1991–2000), first president of Russia after the fall of the Soviet Union

Vladimir Putin (1999–2008, 2012–present), president and former prime minister (1999, 2008–2012) of Russia.

ADMINISTRATIVE DIVISIONS

Federal Districts; Capitals

Central; Moscow

Far East; Khabarovsk

North Caucasus; Pyatigorsk

Northwest; Saint Petersburg

Siberia; Novosibirsk

Southern; Rostov-on-Don

Urals; Yekaterinburg

Volga; Nizhniy Novgorod

GLOSSARY

aristocracy

A member of the upper-class nobility between the twelfth and early twentieth centuries.

bicameral

Two separate and distinct lawmaking assemblies in a government.

boyar

A member of a class higher than Russian nobility but below the prince. Boyars were in charge of the civil and military administration of the country.

capitalism

An economic system based on private ownership of companies, along with the distribution of goods; uses a free competitive market.

Communism

An economic system defined by collective ownership of property and the organization of labor for common advantage; a government system in which a single party holds power and the state controls the economy.

greenhouse gases

Gases, such as carbon dioxide, that are created from the burning of fossil fuels and that trap heat from the sun, contributing to climate change.

infrastructure

A country's transportation and communications networks.

Muslim

A follower of Islam, a monotheistic religion based on the belief that the word of God was revealed to the Prophet Muhammad in the seventh century.

pagan

> Someone who believes in a religion that is not one of the main modern religions; relating to an ancient religion that had many gods and praised nature.

privatization

> To transfer an economic enterprise or public utility from state ownership to private ownership.

steppe

> A treeless plain that is often dry and grass covered.

taiga

> A subarctic forest where the trees have needles and produce cones; located south of the tundra in North America, northern Europe, and Asia.

totalitarian

> A centralized government in which a single party without opposition rules over political, economic, and social life.

tsar

> An emperor of Russia before 1917.

tundra

> A treeless plain with permanently frozen subsoil.

ADDITIONAL RESOURCES

SELECTED BIBLIOGRAPHY

"Country Profile: Russia." *Library of Congress—Federal Research Division*. Library of Congress—Federal Research Division, Oct. 2006. Web. 22 May 2012. PDF.

King, Anna. *Russia, Culture Smart!* London: Kuperard, 2008. Print.

Lonely Planet Russia. London: Lonely Planet, 2009. Print.

Schultze, Sydney. *Culture and Customs of Russia.* Westport, CT: Greenwood, 2000. Print.

"The World Factbook: Russia." *Central Intelligence Agency.* Central Intelligence Agency, 9 May 2012. Web. 22 May 2012.

Ziegler, Charles E. *The History of Russia.* London: Greenwood, 1999. Print.

FURTHER READINGS

Armstrong, Scott Daniel. *Russian Snows: Coming of Age in Napoleon's Army.* Pottstown, PA: Red Barn, 2011. Print.

Hesse, Karen. *Letters from Rifka.* Carmel, CA: Hampton-Brown, 2005. Print.

Yelchin, Eugene. *Breaking Stalin's Nose.* New York: Henry Holt, 2011. Print.

WEB LINKS

To learn more about Russia, visit ABDO Publishing Company online at **www.abdopublishing.com**. Web sites about Russia are featured on our Book Links page. These links are routinely monitored and updated to provide the most current information available.

PLACES TO VISIT

If you are ever in Russia, consider checking out these important and interesting sites!

Bolshoi Theater

Tchaikovsky premiered his ballet *Swan Lake* in 1877 at this theater. Now you can catch an opera or ballet in this famous six-tier auditorium.

Red Square and the Kremlin

Red Square and the adjoining fortress of the Kremlin are sites of numerous museums, churches, armories, and towers. Visitors to Lenin's mausoleum can see his preserved body.

The State Hermitage Museum

Dating from the eighteenth century, five buildings make up the State Hermitage Museum. There are more than 3 million items on display, and the Winter Palace alone has more than 1,000 rooms to tour.

SOURCE NOTES

CHAPTER I. A VISIT TO RUSSIA

1. "Russia." *Encyclopædia Britannica.* Encyclopædia Britannica, 2012. Web. 30 May 2012.

2. "Yakutsk: Journey to the Coldest City on Earth." *Independent.* Independent, 21 Jan. 2008. Web. 31 May 2012.

CHAPTER 2. GEOGRAPHY: WORLD'S LARGEST COUNTRY

1. "The World Factbook: Russia." *Central Intelligence Agency.* Central Intelligence Agency, 8 May 2012. Web. 18 June 2012.

2. "Russia." *Encyclopædia Britannica.* Encyclopædia Britannica, 2012. Web. 18 June 2012.

3. "The World Factbook: Russia." *Central Intelligence Agency.* Central Intelligence Agency, 8 May 2012. Web. 18 June 2012.

4. Ibid.

5. "Russia." *Encyclopædia Britannica.* Encyclopædia Britannica, 2012. Web. 18 June 2012.

6. Ibid.

7. *Lonely Planet Russia.* New York: Lonely Planet, 2009. Print. 114.

8. "Kamchatka Peninsula." *Encyclopædia Britannica.* Encyclopædia Britannica, 2012. Web. 19 Sept. 2012.

9. "Russia." *Encyclopædia Britannica.* Encyclopædia Britannica, 2012. Web. 18 June 2012.

10. Ibid.

11. Ibid.

12. "Caspian Sea." *Encyclopædia Britannica.* Encyclopædia Britannica, 2012. Web. 18 June 2012.

13. "Volga River." *Encyclopædia Britannica.* Encyclopædia Britannica, 2012. Web. 20 Sept. 2012.

14. "Russian Federation." *BBC Weather.* BBC, 23 Mar. 2012. Web. 18 June 2012.

15. Cathy Newman. "Russian Summer." *National Geographic.* National Geographic Society, July 2012. Web. 19 Sept. 2012.

16. "Lake Baikal." *UNESCO.* UNESCO World Heritage Centre, 2012. Web. 18 June 2012.

17. Ibid.

18. "Russia." *Weatherbase.* Canty and Associates, n.d. Web. 19 Sept. 2012.

19. "Historic Centre of Saint Petersburg and Related Groups of Monuments." *UNESCO.* UNESCO World Heritage Centre, 2012. Web. 18 June 2012.

20. "The World Factbook: Russia." *Central Intelligence Agency.* Central Intelligence Agency, 31 July 2012. Web. 19 Aug. 2012.

CHAPTER 3. ANIMALS AND NATURE: LIVING IN THE NORTH

1. *Lonely Planet Russia.* New York: Lonely Planet, 2009. Print. 115.

2. "Summary Statistics: Summaries by Country, Table 5, Threatened Species in Each Country." *IUCN Red List of Threatened Species.* International Union for Conservation of Nature and Natural Resources, 2011. Web. 19 Sept. 2012.

3. "The Volga Delta." *UNESCO.* National Heritage Protection Fund, n.d. Web. 19 Sept. 2012. PDF.

4. "Siberian Tiger." *National Geographic*. National Geographic Society, 2012. Web. 20 June 2012.

5. *Lonely Planet Russia*. London: Lonely Planet, 2009. Print. 115.

6. Galya Diment and Yuri Slezkine. *Between Heaven and Hell: The Myth of Siberia in Russian Culture*. New York: St. Martin's, 1993. Print. 75.

7. "Biological Diversity in the Caucasus." *The Encyclopedia of Earth*. Conservation International, 22 Aug. 2008. Web. 19 Sept. 2012.

8. *Lonely Planet Russia*. London: Lonely Planet, 2009. Print. 119.

9. Ibid. 121.

10. Ibid. 120.

11. "Lake Baikal, Russia." *WWF Global*. WWF, n.d. Web. 19 Sept. 2012.

12. *Lonely Planet Russia*. London: Lonely Planet, 2009. Print. 120.

13. Ibid.

14. Ibid.

15. Ibid. 118.

16. "Wrangel Island." *UNESCO*. UNESCO World Heritage Centre, 2012. Web. 18 June 2012.

CHAPTER 4. HISTORY: HOME OF THE TSARS

1. Abraham Ascher. *Russia, A Short History*. Oxford: One World, 2009. Print. 9.

2. Ibid. 16.

3. Ibid. 18.

4. Ibid. 88–89.

5. Ibid. 50–52, 111.

6. Ibid. 112.

7. Ibid. 196.

8. Sydney Schultze. *Culture and Customs of Russia*. Westport, CT: Greenwood, 2000. Print. 16.

9. "Gulag." *Encyclopædia Britannica*. Encyclopædia Britannica, 2012. Web. 20 Aug. 2012.

CHAPTER 5. PEOPLE: PROUD TRADITIONS

1. "The World Factbook: Russia." *Central Intelligence Agency*. Central Intelligence Agency, 20 June 2012. Web. 2 July 2012.

2. Sydney Schultze. *Culture and Customs of Russia*. Westport, CT: Greenwood, 2000. Print. 3.

3. Fred Weir. "Putin Vows to Halt Russia's Population Plunge with Babies, Immigrants." *Christian Science Monitor*. Christian Science Monitor, 14 Feb. 2012. Web. 1 July 2012.

4. Fred Weir. "Russian's Population Decline Spells Trouble." *Christian Science Monitor*. Christian Science Monitor, 18 Apr. 2002. Web. 28 Aug. 2012.

5. "The World Factbook: Russia." *Central Intelligence Agency*. Central Intelligence Agency, 20 June 2012. Web. 30 June 2012.

6. Ibid.

SOURCE NOTES CONTINUED

7. "Tatar." *Encyclopædia Britannica.* Encyclopædia Britannica, 2012. Web. 28 Aug. 2012.

8. "Bashkir." *Encyclopædia Britannica.* Encyclopædia Britannica, 2012. Web. 28 Aug. 2012.

9. *Lonely Planet Russia.* London: Lonely Planet, 2009. Print. 74.

10. "The World Factbook: Russia." *Central Intelligence Agency.* Central Intelligence Agency, 20 June 2012. Web. 30 June 2012.

11. *Lonely Planet Russia.* London: Lonely Planet, 2009. Print. 74.

12. Ibid.

13. Ibid. 76.

14. "Buryat." *Encyclopædia Britannica.* Encyclopædia Britannica, 2012. Web. 29 Aug. 2012.

15. *Lonely Planet Russia.* London: Lonely Planet, 2009. Print. 76.

16. "Tribe." *BBC Two.* BBC, Mar. 2008. Web. 3 July 2012.

17. Ibid.

18. "The World Factbook: Russia." *Central Intelligence Agency.* Central Intelligence Agency, 8 May 2012. Web. 3 July 2012.

19. "Country Guides: Russia." *Washington Post.* Washington Post Company, 2012. Web. 3 July 2012.

20. "The World Factbook: Russia." *Central Intelligence Agency.* Central Intelligence Agency, 8 May 2012. Web. 3 July 2012.

21. "Pogrom." *Encyclopædia Britannica.* Encyclopædia Britannica, 2012. Web. 30 Aug. 2012.

22. "Russia." *Encyclopædia Britannica.* Encyclopædia Britannica, 2012. Web. 3 July 2012.

CHAPTER 6. CULTURE: CELEBRATED ARTS

1. Sydney Schultze. *Culture and Customs of Russia.* Westport, CT: Greenwood, 2000. Print. 112.

2. Chris Gaylord. "How Peter Carl Fabergé Turned Easter Eggs into Precious Art." *Christian Science Monitor.* Christian Science Monitor, 30 May 2012. Web. 6 July 2012.

CHAPTER 7. POLITICS: FROM COMMUNISM TO DEMOCRACY

1. Natalya Kovalenko. "Vladimir Putin's Biography." *Voice of Russia.* Voice of Russia, 7 May 2012. Web. 8 July 2012.

2. "Country Profile: Russia." *Library of Congress—Federal Research Division.* Library of Congress—Federal Research Division, Oct. 2006. Web. 22 May 2012. PDF.

3. Ibid.

4. Ibid.

5. Ibid.

6. Elise Labott. "Clinton Cites 'Serious Concerns' about Russian Election." *CNN World.* CNN, 6 Dec. 2011. Web. 8 July 2012.

7. Ellen Barry. "After Election, Putin Faces Challenges to Legitimacy." *New York Times.* New York Times, 5 Mar. 2012. Web. 30 Aug. 2012.

CHAPTER 8. ECONOMICS: RICH IN RESOURCES

1. "Russia." *Encyclopædia Britannica.* Encyclopædia Britannica, 2012. Web. 9 July 2012.

2. "The World Factbook: Russia." *Central Intelligence Agency.* Central Intelligence Agency, 20 June 2012. Web. 9 July 2012.

3. Ibid.

4. Ibid.

5. Ibid.

6. Ibid.

7. Ibid.

8. Ibid.

9. Ibid.

10. Ibid.

11. Russell Pittman. "Blame the Switchman? Russian Railways Restructuring after Ten Years." *Economic Analysis Group.* Department of Justice, Feb. 2011. Web. 9 July 2012.

12. Ibid.

13. "The World Factbook: Russia." *Central Intelligence Agency.* Central Intelligence Agency, 20 June 2012. 9 July 2012.

14. Ibid.

15. Ibid.

16. "Russian Federation." *UNESCO.* UNESCO World Heritage Centre, 2012. Web. 9 July 2012.

17. Ksenia Nekhorosheva. "Russian Tourism—Rich in Heritage, Poor in Income." *RIA Novosti.* RIA Novosti, 13 May 2011. Web. 9 July 2012.

18. "Russia." *Encyclopædia Britannica.* Encyclopædia Britannica, 2012. Web. 20 Sept. 2012.

19. *Lonely Planet Russia.* London: Lonely Planet, 2009. Print. 748.

20. Douglas Busvine. "Analysis: Putin Disavows, but Won't Ditch, State Capitalism." *Reuters.* Thomson Reuters, 23 June 2012. Web. 11 July 2012.

21. "Organized Crime." *Encyclopædia Britannica.* Encyclopædia Britannica, 2012. Web. 20 Sept. 2012.

CHAPTER 9. RUSSIA TODAY

1. Cathy Newman. "Russian Summer." *National Geographic.* National Geographic Society, July 2012. Web. 31 Aug. 2012.

2. "Background Note: Russia." *US Department of State.* US Department of State, 19 Mar. 2012. Web. 13 July 2012.

3. "Russia: World Bank Data." *Trading Economics.* Trading Economics, 2012. Web. 2 July 2012.

4. Eugene Scott. "Gorbachev Discusses Future of Russian in Phoenix Speech." *AZCentral.com.* AZCentral.com, 28 Apr. 2012. Web. 31 Aug. 2012.

5. "The World Factbook: Russia." *Central Intelligence Agency.* Central Intelligence Agency, 20 June 2012. Web. 9 July 2012.

INDEX

INDEX CONTINUED

PHOTO CREDITS

2495